MW00908587

JUMBO JACK'S COOKBOOKS
AUDUBON MEDIA CORPORATION
301 BROADWAY • AUDUBON IA 50025
1-800-798-2635

The

I-GOT-FUNNER-THINGS-
TO-DO-THAN-COOKIN'
COOKBOOK

by
Louise Anderson Lum

Quixote Press
1854 - 345th Ave.
Wever, IA 52658
800-571-2665

* * * * * * * * *

Quixote Press
1854 - 345th Ave.
Wever, IA 52658
800-571-2665

PRINTED
IN
U.S.A.

INTRODUCTION

Sorry, but I got funner things to do than write a silly introduction.

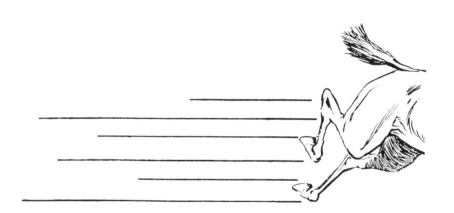

Dedication

—to Margaret and Helen Lum

FOREWORD

TABLE OF CONTENTS

Clowin' Around is Funner Than Cookin'

Now, everybody knows that there is just plain few things that can beat good cookin'.

And really good cookin' is what you get when you use just a few ingredients. The best cookin' of all is what you get when you have only three or four things to put in the pot. If you figure the four, then add one more just to allow for exceptions, that leaves five ingredients at the most. Five's enough, and more than enough in lots of cases.

But, back to what can beat good cookin'. To some extent, that's pretty judgmental. Some folks would put playing bridge ahead of good eats. I love to play bridge, but I wouldn't go so far as to put it out ahead of good cookin'.

Other folks tend to get all teary eyed about fishing or traveling, or whatever. Then there is a thing or two that we'd all agree on, but I'm not going to go into that, this being a family cookbook and all.

The thing is, doing your cooking using this Five-or-Fewer cookbook will give you the time and energy to do those funner things.

Appetizers and Beverages

Iowa Boy Oyster Tomatoes

Cherry tomatoes
Salt

Parsley, chopped
1 can smoked oysters

Wash and dry cherry tomatoes. Split each one to within ¼-inch of the bottom. Squeeze apart, salt and insert an oyster in each one. If oysters are large, cut them in half.

Place on serving dish and sprinkle with parsley.

Brookfield Bacon Dip

1 C. mayonnaise
1 C. sour cream
¼ C. cooked, crumbled,
  very crisp bacon

¼ C. grated horseradish
¼ C. finely chopped red
  or green bell pepper

Stir all ingredients until well mixed. Makes 2 cups.

Singin' is funner than cookin'

Low Calorie Milk Shake

1½ C. skim milk
11 to 12 drops liquid sweetener

2 peaches or ½ C. blueberries
10 ice cubes

Blend in electric mixer on high for one to two minutes. Other flavorings could be 2 teaspoons instant coffee, 1 banana, ½ C. pineapple, or 1 heaping teaspoon orange juice concentrate.

Bingled Cherries

2 C. fresh black bing
   cherries with stems

1 C. dry white wine

Wash cherries and place in glass (not metal) bowl. Pour wine over cherries and refrigerate for 7 to 8 hours. Drain before serving.

Aunt Jennie's Pickled Onions

3½ lbs. onions
3 C. sugar

1¾ C. vinegar

Peel onions and slice very thin; separate rings. Combine sugar and vinegar in plastic or glass container. Stir to dissolve sugar. Add onion rings and mix well. Refrigerate covered for 24 hours. Adjust sugar or vinegar, if necessary.

If you have cucumbers from the garden, slice several very thin and toss them in the bowl, too. These are great served with meat, or drained for sandwiches. A real zinger with an otherwise bland meal.

Yo-Ho-Ho Watermelon Tipsy

1 watermelon
1 C. grapefruit juice

⅓ C. sugar
½ C. rum

Cut off top ¼ of the watermelon. Remove all the watermelon meat and make a sawtooth design on the edge of the large part of the melon. Remove seeds from enough melon to puree one cup of juice. Bring grapefruit juice to a boil and add sugar; stir to dissolve and cool. In a bowl combine juices and rum.

Shape the rest of the watermelon into melon balls and return to melon. Cover with juice.

Top melon with plastic wrap. Refrigerate 4 to 6 hours or overnight. Use more rum if you want to, I don't care.

Bishop Hill Milk Shake

1 C. milk
2 T. sugar

1 C. crushed fresh or
    frozen strawberries
1 C. vanilla ice cream

Combine the milk, sugar and strawberries in a mixer bowl; beat at high speed. Add ice cream and beat to blend. Great on a hot day!

Cheese and Ham Ball

2 (8 oz. ea.) pkgs. cream
    cheese (softened)
1 pkg. pressed ham
    (ground or minced)

2 green onions with tops (minced)
⅓ tsp. garlic salt
Chopped nuts

Combine all ingredients, except chopped nuts. Shape into ball and roll in chopped nuts. Refrigerate and remove about ½ hour before serving.

Amish Glogg

4 C. apple juice
1½ tsp. whole cloves

4 (1-inch) pieces cinnamon stick
5 whole allspice

Tie the spices in a piece of cheesecloth. Bring the juice to a boil and add the spice bag. Simmer for 5 minutes. Remove the spices. Cool juice and refrigerate covered overnight. Serve hot.

Traditionally a mug of glogg would be heated with a red-hot polker. Since most of us don't have stove pokers these days we'll just have to make-do with a pan on the stove or microwave it.

Monkey Milk Shake

1 C. milk
¾ C. vanilla ice cream
½ tsp. sugar
4-inch piece VERY ripe banana

In blender buzz milk, ice cream, and sugar until smooth. Then add the banana slices a few at a time and blend well. Serve immediately.

Sneaky Peach Punch

8 ripe peaches
2 bottles dry white wine (chilled)
4 maraschino cherries

Pour boiling water over the
peaches and let stand about ¾
minute. Remove peaches with
slotted spoon. Skins will peel
off readily.

Put peaches into a clear glass
pitcher. Pour wine over peaches
immediately to prevent
discoloration. Refrigerate for 3
hours so peaches will flavor the
wine.

To serve, place pitcher on the
dinner table. As wine is
poured, add additional chilled
wine.

Peaches can be served sliced
over vanilla pudding or ice
cream for an elegant dessert.

Ridin' is funner than cookin'

Iced Tea

1 gallon of cold water   8 tea bags

Place the tea bags in a glass one-gallon container and fill the jar with cold water. Place out-of-doors in the direct sun and leave for a few hours or until it's the strength you like it.

Bradley Watermelon Balls

2 C. watermelon balls
1 C. lime sherbet
4 lemon slices

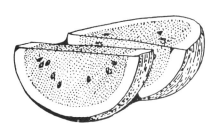

Place melon balls in four serving dishes. Top each serving with a scoop of lime sherbert. Garnish with a lemon slice.

Melon Balls in Wine

2 (10 oz. ea.) pkgs. frozen   3 tsp. sugar
   mixed melon balls or   1 C. dry white wine
   4 C. fresh melon balls

Completely thaw melon balls. When melon balls are at room temperature; drain well. Place fruit in large bowl; sprinkle with sugar and add wine. Chill in refrigerator, turning occasionally. Serve in compote with toothpicks to spear.

Nauvoo Blue Cheese Dip

1½ C. sour cream
3 ozs. crumbled Nauvoo
   blue cheese
1 tsp. chopped parsley

1 tsp. Worcestershire sauce
Optional: 1 clove garlic
   (minced)

Combine the blue cheese and sour cream and blend until smooth. Add the parsley, Worcestershire sauce and if desired, the garlic. Mix well and serve with crackers, chips, or raw vegetables.

I use blue cheese in a lot of things as the factory where it's made is about 10 miles from where I live, so I got a lot of super recipes of the company. You'll come across more of them later.

Creamy Beef Log

1 small jar dried beef,
   chopped
8 oz. pkg. softened cream
   cheese
1¼ C. Cheddar cheese,
   shredded
1 T. horseradish
¾ C. chopped nuts

Combine all ingredients except nuts.
Form into log, then roll in chopped
pecans. Serve on crisp bread or crackers.

Blender Artichoke Dip

1 (12 oz.) carton cottage cheese
4 canned-in-water artichoke
  hearts
1/8 tsp. dill weed

¼ tsp. Tabasco sauce
1 T. mayonnaise

Drain artichokes and rinse. Place all ingredients in the blender. Operate on slow speed, pushing food down until well blended. Switch to high for 40 to 50 seconds. Serve with your choice of raw vegetables.

Chili Dip for Shrimp

1 C. chili sauce
1 tsp. grated horseradish

1 tsp. chopped parsley

Combine ingredients and refrigerate until serving time.

Bud's Spuds

1 dozen VERY small new potatoes
¼ C. sour cream or yogurt
1 T. grated carrot

1 T. chopped green onion & tops
4 slices bacon,
  crisp & crumbled

Boil the potatoes until tender. When cool, peel and slice into halves. Using a teaspoon, hollow out centers. Stir together sour cream, carrot, and onion. Fill potatoes with this mixture and top with crumbled bacon. Serves 3 to 4.

Fantan Anchovy Snacks

Eggs, hard-cooked
Firm, thin, brown bread
Butter, softened

Mayonnaise
Anchovy fillets, canned, rolled
   with a caper in the center

Slice eggs with egg slicer if you have one. If not, use a paring knife. Using largest egg slice as guide, cut rounds of bread slightly larger than the egg slice. Butter bread and spread with mayonnaise. Top each round with an egg slice. Place a rolled anchovy on top of each egg slice.

Place on serving dish and decorate with parsley sprigs or pimiento, if desired.

Egg Salad

4 eggs, hard-cooked and chopped
4 T. green pepper
2 tsp. grated onion

2 tsp. chopped parsley
2 T. mayonnaise

Toss all ingredients until thoroughly blended. Refrigerate at once. Use on either crackers or party rye bread.

Ella's Dip for Apple or Pear Slices

1 (8 oz.) pkg. cream cheese,
    softened
½ C. brown sugar
¼ C. powdered sugar
¾ tsp. vanilla

Blend all ingredients together using the electric mixer. Store covered overnight in refrigerator. Delicious with apple slices.

Adding a little vinegar to water used to boil hard-cooked eggs will keep them from ''running'' if a shell cracks.

Fresh Fruit Medley

2 large apples, red or yellow   2 grapefruit
2 large pears   ½ lb. cherries with stems
2 oranges

Slice apples and pears. Dip in Fruit Fresh if not using right away. Slice oranges and section grapefruit. Clean cherries and drain. Pat dry with paper towels.

Heap the cherries in the center of a serving plate. Arrange fruit slices around the cherries.

If you're not on a diet, serve with any fruit salad dressing. Serves 6.

Onion-Curry Dip

1 pkg. dried green onion
   soup mix
1 C. plain yogurt

1 tsp. curry powder
½ tsp. onion salt

Combine all ingredients in a bowl. Refrigerate 2 to 3 hours before using. This can be thinned with a little milk or cream if a thinner dip is preferred.

Serve with raw vegetables. Makes about 1 cup.

Orange-Raisin Topper for Fruits and Vegetables

1 orange, not peeled
½ C. walnuts
2 C. yellow raisins

½ C. low-cal salad
   dressing or mayonnaise

Cut orange into quarters; remove seeds. Buzz orange and nuts in food processor until chopped fine. Add the mayonnaise and raisins. Process until raisins are finely chopped. Store in covered container. Freezes well for 2 months.

Before using, allow relish to thaw in refrigerator for 3 to 4 hours. Pile on apple, pear and orange slices, celery, or carrot sticks.

Party Punch

2 qts. apple juice
2 qts. orange juice

1 liter ginger ale
1 qt. orange sherbert

Combine well-chilled liquids in punch bowl. Add small scoops of orange sherbet. Will serve 80 to 100 people.

Goldfish Bowl

1 (11 oz.) box oyster crackers
12 oz. Pepperidge Farm
  Goldfish crackers
1 tsp. dill weed

1 pkg. Original Hidden Valley
  Ranch House salad
  dressing mix
½ C. vegetable oil

Pour crackers into large bowl, add dressing mix and dill weed. Drizzle oil over crackers and toss to mix well. Pour crackers onto baking sheet and place in 175° oven until crackers are heated through. Cool and store in tight container.

Flyin' is Funner Than Cookin'

Tropical Float

2 C. pineapple juice
4 C. orange juice

½ C. lime juice
1 pt. orange juice

Combine juices and chill. Pour in glass and add a scoop of sherbet.

Broiled Oyster Snacks

24 oysters
¼ tsp. salt
2 T. chopped parsley

¼ tsp. paprika
8 slices bacon
  (room temperature)

Sprinkle cleaned oysters with salt, parsley, and paprika. Cut bacon strips into 3 pieces. Wrap bacon around each oyster and secure with toothpicks. Broil about 5 inches from heat source for 6 to 8 minutes. Turn and broil an additional 6 to 8 minutes until bacon is crisp. Serves 6 to 7.

Pilot Grove Braunsweiger Snacks

1 C. braunsweiger
½ C. chopped, stuffed olives
  (reserve several whole olives)

¼ C. plus 2 T. chili sauce
1 tsp. minced onion
Party rye bread

Mash braunsweiger and combine with olives, chili sauce and onion. Pile on party rye and top with slice of stuffed olive. Makes about 1 ½ cups.

Thousand Island Dip for Raw Vegetables

8 oz. pkg. cream cheese
⅓ C. Thousand Island
  salad dressing

2 T. catsup
3 tsp. minced onion

Combine all of the ingredients and chill. Serve with raw sliced carrots, celery, green peppers, cucumbers, and mushrooms.

Ham Olive Spread

1 C. ground cooked ham
⅔ C. chopped nuts
½ C. stuffed olives,
  sliced

Mayonnaise
Party rye bread or
  toast triangles

Toss all ingredients with enough mayonnaise to moisten. Serve on party rye bread or toast triangles.

Fruit Dip Raskas

1 C. marshmallow creme
1 C. (8 oz.) cream cheese,
  softened

Apples, unpeeled or any
  fruit you have on hand (sliced)

Whip marshmallow creme and cream cheese together. Neighborhood kids gave this a seal of approval as an after-school snack.

Peanutty Ham Spread

1 C. salted peanuts,
  finely chopped
1 C. cooked and minced ham

1 T. onion, chopped
Mayonnaise

Place peanuts, ham, and onions in a bowl. Toss with just enough mayonnaise to moisten. Serve on crackers.

Garlic Pecans

4 C. pecans
½ stick margarine or butter
2 tsp. Worcestershire sauce

¼ tsp. garlic salt
Dash red pepper

Melt butter or shortening. Combine all ingredients in a shallow pan. Toast in 250° oven 50 to 60 minutes.

Mackinaw Trail Mix

1 C. chocolate chips
1 C. dry roasted peanuts
1 C. raisins

1 C. chopped dried apricots
1 C. almonds or cashews

Combine all ingredients. Carob may be substituted for the chocolate. Store in an airtight container.

Mike's Midnight Snack

4 hard-cooked eggs,
  finely chopped
½ C. chopped onion

1 (2 oz.) can anchovy fillets
1 T. butter or margarine
2 T. finely chopped parsley

Chop anchovies. Melt butter in a heavy skillet and fry onions until a light golden brown. Add chopped anchovies and cook for 1 minute; carefully stir in chopped eggs and heat until warm. Pour into a small bowl and sprinkle with chopped parsley.

Serve this on hot buttered toast triangles or Wasa bread. Wasa is a crisp Swedish rye bread available at even most small-town grocery stores. Sometimes you'll find it with the crackers, sometimes in the foreign foods department, and sometimes only the manager knows where it is. Keep looking.

That's Mike on the right.

Pooh Bah Chili DIp

1 (8 oz.) pkg. cream cheese
1 (15½ oz.) can chili
  WITHOUT beans

⅓ C. sharp Cheddar cheese,
  shredded
1/8 tsp. Tabasco sauce,
  or to taste

Mix cream cheese and chili in a large saucepan. Add Cheddar cheese and Tabasco. Heat slowly to simmering, stirring occasionally. Serve hot with corn chips for dipping.

Billiards are Funner' Than Cookin'

Ol' Timey Pimiento Cheese Spread

1 lb. Cheddar cheese, grated
⅓ C. finely chopped sweet pickle

1 C. mayonnaise
1 (4 oz.) jar pimiento with juice

Combine all ingredients anad beat with electric mixer. Continue whipping until mixture is creamy.

Serve on crackers or spread on bread for sandwiches. Use square bread and slice each sandwich into 3 pieces for your buffet supper.

Snappy Blue Cheese Beef Balls

1 (5 oz.) pkg. smoked sliced beef
1 (8 oz.) pkg. cream cheese, softened
2 T. crumbled Nauvoo blue cheese

1 T. minced onion
1 T. prepared horseradish, drained
Optional: Chopped parsley

Shred beef in blender or chop finely. Mix cream cheese and blue cheese; add shredded beef, onion, and horseradish. Chill for 30 minutes for ease of handling.

Form into balls using 1 T. of mixture for each one. I hope you roll these in chopped parsley as it gives them some color. Refrigerate until ready to serve. Makes 24 balls.

This can be used as a dip by adding 2 T. of cream to the mixture.

River Run Clam Dip

1 (3 oz.) pkg. cream cheese,
  softened
1 (8 oz.) can minced clams

1 tsp. dry mustard
¼ tsp. salt
½ tsp. minced onion

Combine all the ingredients and heat over boiling water. Serve warm over candle flame or in chafing dish.

This is excellent with crackers or chips.

Big Wheel Cheese Dip

½ C. dairy sour cream or yogurt
1 (1.5 oz.) pkg. cheese sauce mix
4 hard-cooked eggs,
  finely chopped
¼ C. drained, canned, chopped
  green chilies
¼ C. chopped green onions with tops

In a medium bowl, blend together sour cream and cheese sauce mix. Stir in remaining ingredients. Cover and chill to blend flavors. Makes about 2 cups.

Four-Aces Onion Chips

½ C. butter
8 oz. sharp Cheddar cheese,
    grated
2 T. plus tsp. dry onion soup mix

1 C. all-purpose flour
½ C. chopped nuts

Have butter and cheese at room temperature; cream together. Add onion soup, flour, and nuts to make a very stiff dough. Turn dough onto lightly floured board and shape into 1½-inch rolls. Wrap in aluminum foil and refrigerate for 3 to 4 hours. Using an electric knife, slice ¼-inch thick. Bake in preheated 375° oven for 12 to 15 minutes or until light brown. When cool, store in a tight container.

Pome Nectar

4 lbs. apples, cored & sliced
2½ qts. water

2 C. sugar

Place the fruit and 1 cup of water in a large kettle. Bring to a boil and simmer for 10 to 15 minutes until the apples are tender. Press through a sieve.

Heat the remaining 1½ C. water with the 2 C. sugar, stirring constantly until sugar dissolves. Then boil rapidly for 2 to 3 minutes.

Measure the apple puree. Add an equal amount of the sugar syrup. Cool and process a small amount at a time in the blender. Then bring the nectar to a fast boil. Strain through several layers of cheesecloth.

Pour into sterilized jars and seal. Process in boiling water for 15 minutes.

Of course you knew all the time that pome is just a two-bit word for apple.

Breads and Sandwiches

Anson's Corn Festival Biscuits

¾ stick butter or margarine
1½ C. Bisquick biscuit mix
  (no cholesterol here)

1 (8½ oz.) can cream style
  corn

Melt the butter or margarine in a cookie sheet with sides. Stir the corn and biscuit mix together. Drop by teaspoons into the melted shortening; turn to coat the other side. Bake at 400° for 20 minutes or until nicely browned. Makes 8 to 10.

Swimmin' is funner than cookin'.

Classic Baking Powder Biscuits From Scratch
(In case you run out of biscuit mix)

2 C. all-purpose flour   4 T. solid shortening
3 T. baking powder   ½ to ¾ C. milk
¾ tsp. salt

Sift together baking powder and flour. Using a pastry blender or fork, cut shortening into the flour mixture until it looks like coarse crumbs. Pour on lightly floured board and knead for a few minutes. Roll dough ¾-inch thick, cut with biscuit cutter, and place on greased pan. Bake in preheated 450° oven. Makes 10 biscuits.

To Have Really Piping Hot Biscuits

Place the cut unbaked biscuits on a baking tin and store in the refrigerator for up to 60 minutes.

To Freeze Unbaked Biscuits

Place cut out biscuits on a baking tin and freeze solid. Store the frozen biscuits in a heavy plastic bag. Bake what you need in a 450° oven for 15 to 20 minutes.

To Use Up Leftover Biscuits

Split biscuits, spread with butter; add a sprinkle of sugar and cinnamon. Bake in hot oven until tops are brown. When my girls were little, they loved these for breakfast.

To Serve Leftover Biscuits with Spaghetti or Meat

Split biscuits, butter and shower with garlic salt or finely chopped garlic. Place under broiler or in hot oven.

Biscuit Mini-Pizzas

½ lb. hamburger
1 can biscuits
1 (small) can pizza sauce

⅔ C. cheese (grated)
½ C. onion (chopped)

Fry hamburger until not quite done; drain.

Stretch each biscuit to desired size; place on a cookie sheet. Top each biscuit with pizza sauce, hamburger, onion, and grated cheese. Bake at 375° for 10 to 15 minutes.

Breadsticks

2 C. flour
¼ tsp. baking powder
½ tsp. salt

4 tsp. butter
2 to 3 T. boiling water

Sift together dry ingredients. Using hands, rub in fat; add water sparingly to make a stiff dough. Knead on floured board until smooth.

Break off small pieces of dough and roll between palms until slightly larger than a lead pencil and about 8 inches long.

Place on lightly greased baking sheet. Bake in preheated 325° oven for about 10 minutes. Sticks should be hard and lightly browned. Cool before storing in airtight container.

Brown Sugar Bread

2¼ C. light brown sugar
4 eggs
2 C. self-rising flour, sifted

1½ C. walnuts (chopped)
2½ tsp. vanilla

Beat brown sugar and eggs together. Put in double boiler over hot water until sugar melts, stirring occasionally. Pour into bowl and add flour, nuts, and flavoring. Pour into 10x14-inch greased pan. Bake at 350° for 20 to 25 minutes.

Chicago Dog

Place your cooked hot dog on a poppy seed bun and top with:

Yellow mustard
Dark green relish
Chopped raw onion

Tomato slices
Dash of celery salt

This is straight from the National Hot Dog and Sausage Council in Chicago, so it has to be authentic! Ask any native of the windy city.

Corn Dodgers

1 C. white cornmeal
¼ tsp. salt

2 T. margarine, melted
Cold water

Combine cornmeal, salt, and margarine. Slowly add enough water to so dough will hold its shape. Pat into biscuits and drop into fast-boiling pot likker. Simmer, covered for 20 to 25 minutes. Serve with greens.

In case you don't know, pot likker is the juice left in the pot after you've cooked turnip greens.

Corned Beef Sandwiches

1 (12 oz.) can corned beef
2 T. chopped onion
3 T. chopped red or green bell pepper
¾ C. chili sauce
2 T. cooking oil

Heat the oil in a skillet; cook onion and pepper until soft, but not brown. Add corned beef and mash to break up; stir in chili sauce.

Cook and stir over low heat until heated. Serve on buns.

Makes 8 sandwiches.

Eatin' is Funner Than Cookin'.

Basic Muffins

2 C. self-rising flour
2 T. sugar
½ C. shortening
1 egg (beaten)
¾ C. milk

Cut shortening into flour until it
looks like little peas. Makes a
hollow in the center; add milk and
beaten egg. Stir briefly — batter
should be lumpy.

If you want to use paper muffin
cups, go ahead, but I prefer
greasing the pans to get a nice brown crust that isn't pulled off. Of course,
if you do this, you will be adding another ingredient.

Fill muffin cups two-thirds full and bake at 400° for 20 to 25 minutes. Makes
10 muffins.

Vary this basic recipe by adding ⅓ to ½ cup fresh or dried chopped fruit,
crumbled bacon or nuts.

Easy English Muffin Pizzas

English muffins, split
Pizza sauce, canned
Cooked sausage, hamburger or
   pepperoni slices

Mozzarella cheese,
   grated
Onion, chopped

Place muffins on lighlty oiled baking sheet. Spoon on pizza sauce and your choice of toppings. Sprinkle with cheese. Bake at 350° until heated through and cheese is melted.

Frenchtown Toast

½ C. milk
2 eggs (beaten)
1 T. sugar

6 to 8 slices of bread
Bacon fat or oil for frying

Combine milk, eggs, and sugar. Dip both sides of bread into the egg mixture. Fry in sizzling bacon fat or oil until brown. Turn and brown the other side. Nice served with maple syrup or honey. Serves 3 to 4.

Flirtin' over the phone is more fun than cookin'.

(39)

Get-Well-Quick Milk Toast

1 THICK slice HOMEMADE bread   ¾ C. hot milk
Butter   Optional: sugar & 1 drop vanilla

Toast bread nice and brown. Butter and place in a shallow soup bowl. Pour hot milk over toast and serve at once.

This was the first food given to convalescents when I was growing up. Sometimes we had it for Sunday night supper.

Sesame Bread Sticks Parmesan

12 slices square sandwich bread   3 T. sesame seeds
¼ C. butter, melted   4 T. onion, minced
¼ C. Parmesan cheese

Remove crusts from bread. Cut each slice into 4 long pieces and place on baking sheet. Using pastry brush, brush with butter. Then sprinkle with cheese, sesame seeds, and onion. Bake at 350° for 12 to 15 minutes. Makes 4 dozen.

(40)

Lightning Down River Dumplings

2 C. biscuit mix   ⅔ C. milk

Stir together biscuit mix and milk. Drop by spoonful on top of hot, done stew. Cook uncovered for 10 minutes. Cover and cook another 10 to 12 minutes.

Lovington Scones

1 C. buttermilk   2 tsp. baking soda
2 C. flour   ½ tsp. salt
½ C. wholewheat flour

Dissolve the soda in 2 T. buttermilk. Stir the flour into the rest of the buttermilk to form a soft dough. Add the salt and soda, mixing thoroughly. Turn dough on to a floured surface and roll lightly. Cut into squares or pie-shaped pieces. Place on greased baking sheet and bake at 400° for 15 minutes. Serve hot.

(41)

Monkey Bread

4 cans (10 count) biscuits
1½ C. brown sugar
1 T. cinnamon
1 C. nuts, chopped fine
1½ sticks margarine or butter

Cut each biscuit in 4 pieces. Combine sugar, cinnamon, and nuts. Roll each biscuit piece in sugar mixture and place half of them in greased Bundt pan. Pour half of margarine or butter over this. Add remaining coated dough balls; pour remaining margarine over top.

Bake in preheated 350° oven for 40 to 45 minutes.

Oak Lawn Cinnamon Toast

2 T. sugar
2 tsp. cinnamon

4 slices whole wheat bread
Butter, room temperature

Place sugar and cinnamon in small dish and stir together. Toast bread, butter and sprinkle liberally with sugar-cinnamon mixture. Toast can be kept warm in 300° oven.

Old Timey Soul Rolls

2 C. self-rising flour   1 C. milk
4 T. mayonnaise   Grease for pan

Grease 12 medium muffin cups. Stir together ingredients and spoon into pan. Bake at 450° for 10 minutes.

Open Face Sandwiches

6 slices Italian bread   6 very thin slices tomato
6 slices Mozzarella cheese   Mixed Italian herbs
12 anchovies

On each slice of bread place a slice of cheese, 2 anchovies, and tomato slices. Sprinkle with a scant pinch of herbs.

Bake on greased baking sheet at 400° for 8 to 10 minutes. Serve 6.

Pancake Mix

3¾ C. flour   2½ tsp. salt
2 T. baking powder   ⅓ C. sugar

Stir, then sift ingredients to combine and store in airtight container. Makes 4 cups.

To use, combine 2⅓ C. mix and ⅔ C. milk or water. Makes 8 to 10 pancakes.

Parmesan Onion Bread

3 T. chopped onion
½ C. mayonnaise

¾ C. grated Parmesan cheese
1 loaf French bread

Stir together onion, mayonnaise, and cheese. Slice the bread in half, lengthwise. Spread with the onion-cheese mixture. Bake at 375° for 12 to 15 minutes. Cheese should bubble and be lightly browned. Cut into serving-size pieces. Makes 14 to 20 pieces.

Blue Cheese Biscuits

2 C. self-rising flour
¼ C. shortening

½ C. Nauvoo Blue cheese
   crumbles
¾ C. milk (or less)

Cut the shortening into the flour until it looks like coarse crumbs. Add the Blue cheese; add milk to make a soft dough. Knead 12 to 15 times.

Cut with cutter and place on ungreased baking sheet. Bake at 450° for 10 to 12 minutes.

Pecan Waffles

2 C. biscuit mix
1⅓ C. milk
1 egg

2 T. oil or melted butter
½ C. chopped pecans

Combine all ingredients, except nuts. Whip with hand beater or whisk until smooth. Stir in pecans. Pour onto center of hot waffle iron. Cook until steaming stops. Loosen edges with fork and remove carefully. Makes 3 (9-inch) waffles.

Sausage Corn Bread

½ lb. small sausage links   1 T. sausage drippings
1½ C. milk   1 egg
2 C. self-rising cornmeal mixture

Brown sausage and drain. Press with paper towels to extract as much grease as possible. Cut each link sausage into 4 pieces. Place all ingredients in a bowl and stir well. Pour into greased 9-inch round pan. Bake in preheated 375° oven for 35 to 40 minutes. Serves 6 to 8.

Oven Croutons

Slices of bread (stale is best)   Onion salt or seasoned salt
Oil   Optional: Paprika

Brush both sides of bread with oil and cut into ½-inch cubes. Arrange cubes on baking sheet, sprinkle with onion or seasoned salt, and paprika if using it. Bake at 400°, stirring frequently until cubes are brown.

These croutons can be frozen and reheated in the oven just before using.

Sprinkle these on soups and salads.

(45)

Swedish Instant Popovers

1 (9½ oz.) pkg. Buterflake
  recipe pie crust mix

3 eggs
1¼ C. milk

Grease popover or muffin pan with butter. Combine pie crust mix, eggs, and milk. Blend at low speed until ingredients are moistened, then beat 1 minute at medium speed. Batter will be lumpy. Fill muffin cups to within ¼-inch from the top. Bake at 375° for 45 to 55 minutes or a deep golden brown. Remove from pan and serve immediately.

Wheat Germ Gems

1½ C. self-rising flour
⅓ C. wheat germ

¼ C. shortening
¾ C. LESS 1 T. milk

Cut shortening into flour until the mixture looks like coarse bread crumbs. Add wheat germ; stir in milk. Turn mixture onto a lightly floured board and knead 10 to 15 times. Pat dough about ½-inch thick and cut with biscuit cutter. Arrange on ungreased baking sheet. Bake at 450° for 12 to 15 minutes.

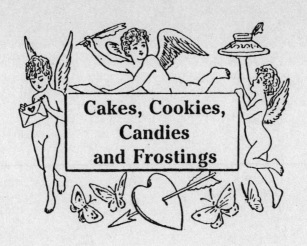

Cakes, Cookies, Candies and Frostings

Black Walnut Butterscotch Clusters

1 pkg. butterscotch pudding, dry
1 C. sugar
2 tsp. butter
½ C. evaporated milk
1½ C. chopped black walnuts or
    other nuts

Combine all ingredients, except nuts. Bring to an easy boil and cook to the soft ball stage which will be 235° to 240° on your candy thermometer. Let cool a big, then beat until it begins to thicken. Stir in nuts and drop from teaspoon onto waxed paper.

Brown Sugar Pecans

1 C. brown sugar
½ C. white sugar
½ C. sour cream
1½ tsp. vanilla
2½ C. chopped pecans

Stir together sugars and sour cream in a saucepan. Cook over low heat, stirring constantly to 277° on a candy thermometer, or until a few drops form a soft ball in a cup of cold water. Pour into bowl, add flavoring and nuts. Stir until nuts are well coated. Drop from teaspoon onto aluminum foil or waxed paper.

Bikin' is funner than cookin'.

Buckeye Balls

2 sticks buter or margarine,
  at room temperature
2 C. peanut butter
6 C. (1½ lbs.) powdered sugar

½ of a 12 oz. pkg. of
  chocolate chips
½ cake of paraffin wax

Combine and knead butter or margarine, peanut butter and sugar. Shape into balls. Combine chocolate chips and paraffin in the top of a double boiler to melt. Pierce each ball with a toothpick and dip into chocolate-paraffin mixture. Place on waxed paper to cool. When chocolate has set pour warm chocolate from a teaspoon to fill holes.

Hide these as they won't last long around the kids.

Orange Glaze

2 C. confectioner's sugar
½ C. hot water

½ tsp. butter
1 tsp. grated orange peel

Combine sugar, butter, and orange peel in a bowl. Add boiling water and stir. Pour over cake or cookies. To thin glaze, add a few drops of hot water and stir well.

Cherry Nut Fudge

2 C. sugar	½ C. chopped maraschino
1 C. heavy cream	cherries
¾ C. chopped nuts	1 tsp. vanilla

Combine sugar and cream in saucepan. Bring to boil over medium heat and add salt. Cook, stirring constantly with a wooden spoon, to softball stage, 230° to 240°. Remove from heat. When almost cold, beat until thick and creamy. Cover with a damp cloth for 30 minutes. With hands, work in vanilla, nuts, and cherries. Line pan with waxed paper and press fondant into pan.

Yes, I know there's one extra ingredients, but you just have to try this.

Carrot Spice Drops

1 pkg. (2-layer) Pillsbury	½ C. cooking oil
carrot 'n spice cake, dry	½ C. applesauce
¾ C. currants or raisins	1 egg

Combine all ingredients in a large mixer bowl. Beat at medium speed for 2 minutes. Using a teaspoon, drop 2 inches apart on a lightly greased baking sheet. Bake at 350° for 12 to 15 minutes. Makes 5½ dozen.

Chocolate Chip Bars

5 T. butter or margarine
½ lb. marshmallows
¾ C. chocolate chips

¾ tsp. vanilla
3½ C. corn flakes or Rice Krispies

Melt marshmallows and butter over boiling water. Remove from the heat and add vanilla. Place the corn flakes or Rice Krispies in a large, buttered bowl. Pour marshmallow mixture over the flakes and stir. Pat mixture into buttered 9x12-inch pan. Press the chocolate chips on top. Cool and cut into bars. Makes 4 dozen small bars.

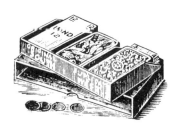

Coconut Shortbread

2 sticks butter
½ C. sugar
2 tsp. vanilla

2 C. all-purpose flour
½ C. flaked coconut

Cream sugar and butter; add vanilla. Stir flour and coconut together and blend with butter-sugar mixture. Dough will be very stiff. Turn dough onto lightly floured surface, divide, and shape into 2 rolls. Refrigerate for 2 to 3 hours, then slice into ¼-inch slices. Place on ungreased baking sheet. Bake at 350° for 15 to 20 minutes. May be sprinkled with powdered sugar, if desired. Makes 2½ dozen cookies.

Constellation Cakes

1½ C. biscuit mix
2 (3 3/8 oz.) pkgs. instant
  pudding, any flavor
2 eggs

¼ C. butter or margarine
Chocolate candy stars or
  Hershey Kisses

Combine biscuit and pudding mixes. Add beaten eggs and melted shortening. Stir to blend. Drop from a teaspoon onto ungreased baking sheet. Bake at 350° for 12 minutes. Remove from the oven and press candy star on top of each cake.

Small chunks of dipping chocolate may be substitued for the stars or Kisses.

Country Bumpkin Candy

1 can condensed milk
(Eagle Brand)
1 (12 oz.) pkg. semi-sweet
chocolate chips
2 T. butter

1¾ C. unsalted dry roasted
peanuts
1 (6½ oz.) pkg. miniature
marshmallows

Place the nuts and marshmallows in a buttered 9x13-inch pan. Heat the butter, chocolate, and milk over low heat until the chocolate is melted. Pour the mixture over the peanuts and marshmallows. When cold, cut into squares. Store in the refrigerator.

Daffodil Cake

3 sticks butter
3½ C. powdered sugar
3¼ C. all-purpose flour
6 large eggs
2 tsp. vanilla

Cream the butter and powdered sugar. Add the flour, eggs, and vanilla to end up with flour. Pour into a greased and floured tube pan. Bake at 350° for 1 hour. An inserted toothpick should come out clean.

Hazlenut Butter Cookies

2 C. flour
1 C. butter (room temp.)
½ C. powdered sugar

¾ tsp. vanilla
Chopped hazelnuts
  (or other nuts)

Combine sugar, butter, flour, and vanilla. Mix well and form into 2-inch long logs. Sprinkle with chopped nuts. Bake at 300° for 10 minutes.

Lemon Anise Bars

3 eggs, separated
½ C. sugar
1 tsp. grated lemon peel

¾ C. plain flour
¾ anise seed

Whip the egg white until stiff; beat the yolks until lemon colored. Slowly beat the lemon peel and sugar into the yolks. Stir the anise seeds with a little flour and fold into egg mixture; fold in the egg whites.

Line a 9-inch pan with a double thickness of waxed paper. Pour in the batter and bake at 375° for 15 to 20 minutes. When cool, cut into squares. Makes 16 bars.

Lemon Balls

1 box (18¼ oz.) lemon cake mix
with pudding
1 stick butter or margarine,
melted (plus 1 T. for greasing pan)

1 C. Rice Krispies cereal
½ C. ground or chopped nuts

Combine all ingredients and shape into balls. Place 2-inches apart on lightly greased cookie sheet. Bake for 10 minutes or until lightly browned. Makes 5 dozen.

Marshmallow Date Crispies

4 T. butter or margarine
½ lb. marshmallows
½ tsp. vanilla

5 C. Rice Crispies
¾ C. chopped dates

Combine the butter and marshmallows over boiling water. Stir frequently until syrupy. Add the vanilla and stir.

Place the Crispies and dates in a large, buttered bowl; toss together. Add the marshmallow mixture and stir. Press into a waxed-paper line pan. When cool, cut into squares. Makes 36 squares.

Easy Peanut Brittle Frosting

1 can (16½ oz.) vanilla frosting
4 T. peanut butter

¾ C. crushed peanut brittle

Combine vanilla frosting and peanut butter in a bowl. This will frost 1 oblong cake or a 2-layer cake. Sprinkle the crushed peanut brittle over the frosting.

Abbie's Apricot Torte

1 pkg. Jiffy 1-layer dark
  fudge cake
1 egg

½ C. water
¾ C. apricot preserves
Whipped topping

Prepare and bake cake according to directions on package. When cool, split each cake in half horizontally. Soften preserves by bringing to a boil or in a microwave oven. When almost cool, spread on bottom half of cake. Cover this with the top half. Cover top of cake with whipped topping or whipped cream.

Keep one of these in the freezer (without the topping) for unexpected guests. Just set out cake and cover with topping before serving. To dress it up, sprinkle whipped topping with a broken toffee bar or two, chocolate curls, nasturtium blossoms, or whatever suits your fancy.

Ginger Pops

1 pkg. gingerbread mix
⅓ C. warm water

1 C. chopped nuts

Combine all ingredients. Shape dough into 1-inch balls. Place 2-inches apart on ungreased cookie sheet. Grease bottom of large glass and flatten cookies. Place in 375° oven for 8 to 10 minutes. Cool cookies 1 minute before removing with a spatula. Cool on wire rack.

Alton Pineapple Cookies

1 stick margarine or butter,
   room temperature
2 eggs
1 (3 oz.) pkg. pineapple gelatin

1 pkg. pound cake mix
1 (8 oz.) can crushed pineapple,
   drained

Combine all ingredients in large mixer bowl. Beat at medium speed for 2 minutes, scraping down sides of bowl with spatula. Drop by teaspoon 2-inches apart on Teflon-coated pan or lightly greased uncoated pan. Bake at 375° for 10 to 12 minutes. Cool for 1 minute before removing from pan. Makes 3½ dozen.

Birthday Ice Cream Cake

1½ pkgs. lady fingers, split
1 to 1½ qts. chocolate ice cream,
   softened

1 to 1½ qts. butter pecan
   ice cream, softened
10 toffee bars, crushed

Arrange the lady fingers (rounded side out) around the sides and bottom of an angel food cake pan. Fill the pan half full with chocolate ice cream. Sprinkle ½ of the crushed toffee bars over the chocolate ice cream.

Spread the butter pecan ice cream over the top of this. Sprinkle with the remaining nut-toffee mixture.

Cover with foil and freeze overnight. Serves 10 to 12.

Butter Nut Bars

1 C. butter, room temperature
1 C. sugar
2 C. flour

1 egg (beaten)
¾ C. chopped walnuts

In mixer bowl beat butter and sugar until light and fluffy. Add flour, ½ C. at a time, beating after each addition. Smooth into ungreased jelly roll pan (15½x10½-inch). Brush dough with egg and sprinkle with nuts. Bake for 20 minutes. Test with toothpick. If toothpick comes out clean, cookies are done. If not, bake another 3 to 5 minutes. Top should be golden brown.

Caramel Frosting

1 (1 lb.) pkg. light-brown sugar
1 C. Half & Half or cream

1 stick butter
1 tsp. vanilla

Cook sugar, cream, and butter to 240° or until a few drops form a soft ball in ½ C. cold water. Remove from heat, add vanilla and beat until it thickens. Frost cake at once.

Cherry Pineapple Cake

1 (1 lb.) can crushed pineapple
1 (1 lb.) cherry pie filling
1½ C. butter or margarine

1 pkg. yellow cake mix
¾ C. chopped walnuts

Pour pineapple and cherry pie filling in an 8x12-inch baking pan. Sprinkle cake mix over fruit; add nuts. Top with pieces of butter or margarine. Bake at 350° for 1 hour.

Chocolate Chip Graham Squares

1½ C. graham cracker crumbs
1⅓ C. flaked coconut
¾ C. chocolate chips

1 (14 oz.) can sweetened
condensed milk

Stir together all ingredients. Batter will be thick. Pour in greased and floured 8x8x2-inch pan. Bake at 350° for 25 to 30 minutes or until a toothpick comes out clean. Cool in pan for 8 minutes. Cut into bars.

Chocolate Glaze

2 sq. (2 oz.) unsweetened
  chocolate
2 T. butter

1½ C. confectoiner's sugar
4 T. milk

Place chocolate and butter in a saucepan and melt over very low heat. Add sugar and stir well. Add heated milk gradually until mixture is thin enough to pour. If necessary, an additional small amount of milk can be added. While still warm, pour over cookies or cake.

Classic Refrigerator Cookies

2 C. brown sugar, packed
2 eggs, beaten
1 C. butter (2 sticks)

3½ C. self-rising flour
¾ tsp. vanilla

Cream butter and sugar; add eggs and beat well. Shape the dough in 3 rolls and wrap in plastic wrap. Refrigerate overnight. Slice in ¼-inch slices and bake at 350° for 8 to 10 minutes.

Cool Kitchen Peanut Butter Fudge

2 sticks butter
1 C. peanut butter

¾ tsp. vanilla
3½ C. powdered sugar

Melt butter and peanut butter together. Stir in powdered sugar and vanilla. Pour onto wax paper and refrigerate. Cut into squares. This keeps best stored in the refrigerator.

Microwave Chocolate Nut Squares

2½ C. chocolate chips
1 square (1 oz.) baking chocolate,
  chopped

1 (14 oz.) can sweetened
  condensed milk
1 C. chopped nuts

Place chocolates in paper dish and cover with plastic wrap. Microwave 3 to 4 minutes on low; stir. If bits are not melted, microwave briefly and test stir again. When melted, pour into mixer bowl, add condensed milk and nuts. Beat until blended. Pour into plastic-lined 8x8x2-inch pan. Chill until firm. Cut into 1-inch squares.

Store in the refrigerator or freeze. Makes 64 pieces.

Mom's Easy Cookies

1 C. sugar
2 C. butter
1 egg, beaten

2⅔ C. flour
Optional: Seeded raisins or
  nut halves

Cream butter and sugar; add beaten egg and stir in flour. Place in a plastic bag and refrigerate for 2 hours before rolling out. Cut with cutters. Bake at 350° for about 10 to 15 minutes before removing from the pan.

Swimmers' Almond Bark Crunch

1 lb. almond bark
1 (18 oz.) jar peanut butter
1 box round, buttery crackers

3 T. solid white shortening
½ C. ground or chopped peanuts

Melt almond bark and shortening over hot water; blend well. Spread peanut butter between 2 crackers. Using tongs, dip crackers in melted almond bark; place on waxed paper. Cool and store in tightly covered container.

No Cook Honey Butter Balls

1 C. peanut butter
1 C. honey
2 C. powdered milk, dry

¾ C. nuts (chopped)
1 C. corn flakes, crushed

Stir together peanut butter and honey. Stir in dry milk and nuts. Shape into balls. Roll in corn flake crumbs. Store these in the refrigerator.

No Sugar Vanilla Cookies

4 oz. cream cheese, softened
2 eggs
1 T. sugar substitute

½ tsp. vanilla
Pam spray

Separate eggs. Beat together cheese, egg yolks, and vanilla. Beat egg white until stiff. Fold 2 mixtures together. Drop from teaspoon onto Pam sprayed cookie sheet. Bake at 350° for 10 to 12 minutes.

Oatmeal Squares

1 C. firmly packed brown sugar
1 stick softened butter or
  margarine

2 C. quick-cooking oatmeal
1 tsp. baking powder
½ C. finely chopped nuts

Combine all ingredients in a mixer bowl. Beat at medium speed for 1 minute. Pour into greased and floured 8x8x2-inch pan. Bake at 350° for 25 minutes. These ''firm-up'' when cooling.

Peanut Butter Cookies

1 pkg. yellow cake mix
1 C. peanut butter
½ C. cooking oil
2 T. water
2 eggs

Combine all ingredients in mixing bowl and stir well. Mix at high speed for 2 minutes. Drop by teaspoons on ungreased cookie sheet. Flatten slightly with fork tines. Bake at 350° for 12 to 14 minutes.

Pink Petal Cake

1 pkg. white cake mix
1 (3 oz.) pkg. cherry Jello
  (or any other flavor)

¾ C. water
½ C. salad oil
4 eggs, not beaten

Combine all ingredients in large bowl. Beat 5 minutes. Mixture should be smooth. Line bottom of 10-inch tube pan with paper. Pour in batter and bake at 350° for 50 to 55 minutes. Inserted toothpick should come out clean. Cool in pan for 15 minutes. Remove and cool on cake rack.

Raisin Clusters

8 oz. chocolate bark, melted
¼ C. cream

1 C. raisins
½ C. chopped nuts

Line 8x8x2-inch pan with plastic wrap. Combine all ingredients and pour into pan. Allow to cool and refrigerate. Cut into squares.

Red Raspberry Crescents

½ lb. butter (2 sticks)
½ lb. cream cheese, softened
2 C. flour

Red raspberry preserves
Flour for rolling out

Cream together first 3 ingredients until free of lumps. Refrigerate in a plastic bag overnight. Roll the dough out on a floured surface until 1/8-inch thick; cut into 2-inch squares. Place ½ teaspoon raspberry jam in center of each cookie. Fold and turn corners to form crescents. Bake at 400° until golden brown.

Refrigerator Oat Bars

2 C. chocolate chips
¾ C. peanut butter

2½ C. round oat cereal
½ C. chopped nuts

Combine chocolate chips and peanut butter in small saucepan. Stir over very low heat until blended and smooth. Remove from heat; stir in cereal and nuts and pour into waxed paper lined 8x8x2-inch pan. Refrigerate until firm. Cut into 24 squares.

Boatin' is funner than cookin'

Tote It Along Toffee

1 C. sugar
2 sticks butter
3 T. water

1 tsp. vanilla
Chocolate bars

Combine sugar, butter, and water. Cook for 10 minutes until brown, stirring constantly. Remove from heat and add vanilla. Smooth mixture onto a buttered pan. Lay plain chocolate bars on hot toffee and smooth out with spatula. Crack up.

Savanna Sand Bars

1 can condensed milk
(Eagle Brand)
1 (12 oz.) pkg. chocolate chips,
semi-sweet
2 T. butter

1 ¾ C. dry roasted peanuts,
unsalted
1 (6 ½ oz.) pkg. miniature
marshmallows

Combine butter, chocolate, and milk over very low heat. Pour mixture over peanuts and marshmallows in buttered 9x13-inch pan. When cold, cut into squares. These keep best in the refrigerator.

Sioux Bee Refrigerator Cookies

½ C. peanut butter
¼ C. honey
1 C. flaked coconut

2 C. puffed wheat, sugar-coated,
divided ½ C. & 1½ C.
⅓ C. chopped nuts

Combine peanut butter, honey, and coconut; stir well. Add ½ C. puffed wheat and stir in. Spread remaining cereal on waxed-paper lined plate. Shape mixture into balls with hands and roll in cereal. Refrigerate until firm.

Sorghum Squares

1 C. sorghum syrup
2 C. roasted peanuts,
unsalted, crushed

½ C. coconut
1 tsp. vanilla
4 T. butter

Boil sorghum to 245° to 248° on candy thermometer or until a few drops in a cup of cold water are firm. Remove from heat, stir in butter and vanilla. Add crushed pineapple. Pour into greased pan. While still warm, mark into squares.

Ya' Gotta Try These Nuts

¾ C. brown sugar
1 unbeaten egg white

2½ C. coarsely chopped nuts

Mix the sugar and unbeaten egg white; stir in the nuts. Smooth on ungreased baking sheet. Bake at 275° for 30 minutes. Remove with spatual and break into pieces.

Snowflake Truffles

4 C. shaved or cubed white
   chocolate
⅓ C. butter
½ C. heavy cream (cold)

¾ tsp. orange, lemon, vanilla or
   rum flavoring

Combine white chocolate and butter in the top of a double boiler. Don't allow water to touch the pan. Stir constantly until chocolate and butter are melted. Don't worry if the mixture looks grainy at this point.

Remove the kettle from over the hot water and stir in the cream and flavoring a tablespoon at a time. By the time the last of the cream is added, the graininess should have disappeared. However, in case it hasn't beat in a little more cream, using an electric mixer.

Spoon into 8-inch square pan lined with plastic wrap. When firm, cut into squares. Store this hidden in the back of the refrigerator.

If preferred, the cold candy can be shaped into balls with hands dusted with cornstarch.

Yazoo Cream Cake

4 eggs, separated
1½ C. sugar
½ pt. heavy cream

1 tsp. vanilla
1¾ C. (self-rising) flour

Beat the egg yolks until lemon colored. Add sugar and beat well. Add cream and vanilla and blend at low speed. Add cake flour and mix thoroughly. Beat egg whites until stiff; fold into batter. Pour into greased 9-inch tube pan. Bake at 350° for about 1 hour.

Susan's Rum Balls

1 C. heavy cream
1 lb. semi-sweet chocolate,
  grated

1½ C. chopped walnuts
⅔ C. rum

Bring cream to a boil over medium heat and add grated chocolate; cook and stir with wooden spoon until chocolate is thick and smooth. Remove from heat. When cold, stir in nuts and rum. When firm enough, roll into balls. Roll in grated chocolate or ground nuts, if desired.

Thimble Jam Cookies

1 roll refrigerated sugar   Jam, any flavor
   cookie dough

Slice dough into ¼-inch slices. Place a little jam in center of one slice. Using a floured thimble, cut a hole in the center of a second slice. Place this slice on top of the slice with jam. Seal edges with tines of a fork, then pierce tops. Bake at 375° until nicely browned.

I used mom's leftover pie crust for these when I was a kid. Just moisten the edges, as for a 2-crust pie before putting slices together, then pierce tops to allow steam to escape.

Whipped Cream Frosting

½ pt. (8 oz.) whipping cream
2½ T. sugar
1 tsp. vanilla flavoring
Optional: Food coloring

Cream, bowl, and beaters should be chilled. Whip cream until almost stiff. Add sugar and vanilla and beat until stiff. This will frost the top of a cake. Double the recipe for a 2-layer cake.

One tablespoon of instant coffee can be added to make coffee frosting.

Taylorville Trifle

1 (3½ oz.) pkg. instant
  vanilla pudding
1½ C. milk
1 (7 oz.) pkg. small jelly rolls

2½ C. whipping topping, divided
3 C. sliced strawberries
  (reserve 3 whole ones with
  leaves for garnish)

Prepare the instant pudding with 1½ C. milk. Allow to sit for 10 minutes. Fold in 1 cup of the whipped topping.

Slice each jelly roll into 3 pieces; stand these around the sides of a glass bowl so the red rings show. Put the extra slices on bottom of the bowl.

Spread ½ of the strawberries over the slices in the bottom of the dish. Pour in the pudding mixture. Spread the remaining strawberries over the pudding; spread the rest of the topping over the strawberries. Garnish with reserved berries. Store in the refrigerator. Serves 8.

Date Nut Cookies

2 C. chopped pecans
2 C. chopped pitted dates
2 C. coconut (reserve ½ C.)

¾ C. dark brown sugar
    (packed)
2 eggs (beaten)

Work together nuts, dates, and coconut or put through a food chopper. Combine all ingredients and shape into balls. Roll in reserved coconut. Space 2-inches apart on a greased cookie sheet. Bake at 350° for 10 minutes or until golden brown. Make 3 dozen cookies.

Erma's Rhubarb Cake

4 C. rhubarb (diced)
1 pkg. strawberry Jello

1 C. sugar
1 small pkg. Jiffy cake
1 C. water

Spread ½ rhubarb in bottom of casserole. Sprinkle with ½ of the Jello, sugar, and dry cake mix. Repeat, topping with dry cake mix. Pour the water very slowly over all. Bake at 350° or until nicely browned.

(71)

No Bake Fruit Cake

1 lb. vanilla wafers
3½ C. nuts, chopped
1 lb. yellow raisins

1 can sweetened condensed milk
1 C. candies mixed fruit,
   chopped

Use rolling pin to roll vanilla wafers into crumbs. Combine all ingredients and press into loaf pan. Chill for several hours or overnight.

Plenty good Grahams

4 oz. margarine (1 stick)
½ C. sugar

½ C. nuts (chopped)
Graham crackers

Bring sugar and margarine to a boil. Remove from heat and stir in nuts. Brush on graham crackers. Bake at 350° for 10 minutes.

Lemon Cookies

1½ C. biscuit mix
2 pkgs. lemon pudding, instant
½ C. cooking oil

2 eggs
½ C. sugar

Combine all ingredients, except sugar. Roll dough into small balls and dip in sugar. Place unsugared side down on baking sheet. Flatten cookies slightly with fork. Bake at 350° for 10 to 15 minutes.

(72)

Desserts

Adeline's Mini Cheesecakes

12 vanilla wafers ½ C. sugar
2 (8 oz. ea.) pkgs. cream cheese 2 eggs
1 tsp. vanilla

Line 12-cup muffin tin with foil liners. Place 1 vanilla wafer in each liner. Mix cream cheese, vanilla, and sugar on medium speed until well blended. Add eggs and mix well. Pour over wafers, filling ¾ full. Bake at 325° for 25 minutes. Remove from pan when cool.

If you're in the mood and have the time, these can be dolled up with crushed and sweetened fresh fruit preserves, nuts, chocolate or what have you.

Baked Fruit Medley

1 (20 oz.) can chunk pineapple 2 (11 oz. ea.) cans mandarin
1 (21 oz.) can cherry pie oranges, drained
  filling 1 (12 oz.) pkg. dried prunes

Place all ingredients in a large casserole. Cover and bake in preheated 350° oven for 50 to 60 minutes.

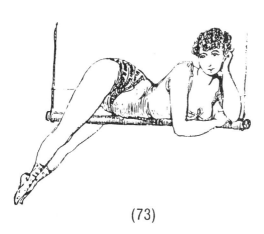

Bavarian Delight

2 C. finely chopped strawberries
1 (3 oz.) box strawberry Jello, dry

1 (8 oz.) container whipped
 topping
1 pt. whipping cream

Beat whipping cream until stiff peaks form. Beat in Jello a small amount at a time. When thoroughly blended, fold mixture with whipped topping; fold in chopped strawberries. Refrigerate for 2 to 3 hours. Serves 6 to 8.

Chocolate Dessert Cups

6 oz. semi-sweet chocolate squares
2 T. solid vegetable shortening

Melt chocolate and shortening over hot water. Using a small pastry brush, paint bottoms, then sides of muffin cups to about ⅓-inch from the top. Refrigerate until firm. Peel paper off and store cups in the refrigerator until ready to use.

These are nice filled with pudding or ice cream.

Dingalings

Melt 12 oz. semi-sweet chocolate in microwave. Gradually stir in 3½ to 4 cups whole wheat flake cereal. Drop by tablespoonfuls onto foil-lined cookie sheets. Refrigerate until firm. Makes about 3 dozen candies.

Banana Graham Dessert

4 C. whipping cream
¾ C. powdered sugar
¾ tsp. rum flavoring

6 to 7 bananas, sliced
54 graham crackers

Whip the cream with flavoring and sugar. On a serving plate arrange 9 crackers in a square. Top with a thin layer of whipped cream, then bananas. Repeat so that top layer is crackers. Then spread cream on sides and top. Chill for 4 to 6 hours. If it suits your fancy, dress this us with nuts, candied fruits or chocolate curls.

Chilled Lime Peaches

1 (30 oz.) can peach halves
3 T. brown sugar

2 T. lime juice
2 T. grated lime peel

Drain peaches, reserving ½ C. of juice. Combine ½ C. peach juice, brown sugar, and lime juice. Bring to boil and simmer for 5 minutes. Place peaches flat side down in a shallow serving dish. Sprinkle with peel. Refrigerate overnight. Serves 7 to 8.

First Lady Cake

Split 1 layer of Jiffy yellow cake to make 2 thin layers. Top bottom layer with strawberry preserves, put on top layer and sprinkle with powdered sugar.

Chocolate Blancmange

4 T. cocoa
4 T. cornstarch
½ C. plus 1 T. sugar

2 C. milk
¾ tsp. vanilla

Combine dry ingredients. Add enough milk to make a paste, then gradually stir in the remaining milk. Cook over very low heat, stirring constantly until thickened and smooth. Add vanilla and pour into serving dishes. Serves 4.

Creme De Menthe Sundae

Chocolate or vanilla ice cream

Creme de Menthe (green)

Place a large scoop of ice cream in a stemmed serving dish. Top with 1 to 2 T. Creme de Menthe. Nice garnished with whipped cream and cherries.

Chocolate Sauce for Ice Cream

2 sq. unsweetened chocolate   1 large can evaporated milk
1 C. sugar   ¾ tsp. vanilla

Melt chocolate with sugar in top of double boiler. Remove from heat and add milk slowly. Return to heat and cook, stirring constantly until thickened.

Fancy Baked Apples

4 apples   4 T. brown sugar
⅓ C. chopped almonds   4 T. chopped nuts
¼ C. raisins

Core but do not cut through the bottom of the apples. Combine the remaining ingredients and fill apples. Add ¼-inch water. Cover and bake at 350° for 30 minutes or until apples are done.

Fruit Delight

1 (10 oz.) pkg. mixed frozen fruit   1 T. grenadine syrup
3 T. cherry-flavored liqueur   1 pt. cherry ice cream

In a glass jar combine fruit, cherry liqueur and grenadine syrup. Cover and refrigerate 4 hours. To serve, spoon fruit into four serving dishes, and top with a scoop of cherry ice cream or raspberry sherbet. Garnish with whipped topping, if desired.

Christmas Sherbet

1 qt. lime sherbert   1 qt. raspberry sherbert

Line a 10x15-inch jelly-roll pan with waxed paper. Extend paper 2-inches beyond both short sides. Place in the refrigerator until chilled. Spread the lime sherbet smoothly in the bottom of the pan. Freeze for 4 hours or until firm. Spread raspberry sherbet over lime; freeze until quite firm, but NOT SOLID, about 2½ to 3 hours.

To roll up: loosen long sides of sherbet from waxed paper. Start with narrow side of paper and roll like jelly roll. Avoid rolling the paper. Place roll seam-side down on serving platter (freezer-proof). Freeze until serving time. Serves 8 to 10.

CHRISTMAS
GREETINGS

Granny Apple Betty

6 Granny Smith apples
1 C. brown sugar (packed)

1 C. flour
½ C. butter or margarine

Peel and quarter the apples; cut into even medium-thick slices. Arrange slices so they overlap in buttered shallow baking dish. With pastry blender or hands, mix together sugar, flour, and butter until crumbly. Distribute evenly over apples and bake in preheated 250° oven for an hour, or until apples are tender. Can be served warm or cold with or without cream.

Ginger Pears

4 pears, peeled & cored
1 T. lemon juice
4 T. brown sugar

4 T. white wine
1 slice fresh ginger root or
   ½ tsp. ground ginger

Place pear halves in a baking dish and sprinkle with the lemon juice and sugar. Smash the ginger with the side of a cleaver and place in baking dish or sprinkle with ground ginger. Add the wine and bake at 350° for 25 to 30 minutes. Serve hot or cold. Serves 4.

Courtin' is Funner than Cookin'.

Greengage Dessert

1 (1 lb. 14 oz.) can greengage
  plums, drained
Cherries, large sweet
  (reserve 6 with stems for garnish)

Whipped cream or
  whipped topping

Seed and halve cherries; stir with plums. Place 1 T. whipped cream in bottom of sherbet glass. Spoon in plum-cherry mixture. Top with whipped cream and garnish with cherry with stem.

Java Coffee Gelatin

1 T. plain gelatin
½ C. cold water
1½ C. strong coffee

¼ C. sugar
1½ tsp. vanilla

Soften the gelatin in cold water; stir mixture into the coffee. Add the sugar and vanilla. Refrigerate until not quite congealed. Whip in the blender until fluffy. Pour into dessert dishes. Serves 4.

Lydia's Lemon Pudding

1 C. sugar
2 T all-purpose flour
2 T. plus 2 tsp. lemon juice

2 eggs, separated
1 C. milk

In top of double boiler stir together sugar, flour, lemon juice, egg yolks, and milk. Whip egg whites until very stiff and fold into lemon mixture. Cover and cook over simmering water for 1 hour. Do not uncover while cooking. Serve warm or cold.

Orange Sauce for Ice Cream

4 large oranges
Water

1 C. sugar
1 C. water

Peel oranges very carefully to avoid including white part of peel; cut peel into very thin julienne strips. Cover with water in heavy saucepan and bring to a boil. Drain rind and repeat the process. This will remove bitterness from the peel.

Bring sugar and water to a boil. When sugar is dissolved, add the orange peel. Cook, stirring occasionally until syrup thickens and peel is tender (about 30 minutes). Remove from heat. When cool, pour into jar and refrigerate. Makes 1 cup. Delicious on ice cream or pudding.

Pineapple Fluff

1 (8 oz.) container whipped
  topping
1 (3 oz.) box raspberry gelatin

¾ C. miniature marshmallows
1¼ C. crushed pineapple
  (undrained)

In a bowl combine whipped topping, dry gelatin, marshmallows, and pineapple. Cover and refrigerate for 3 to 4 hours or overnight.

Minute Mousse

1 (4 oz.) box instant pudding,
  any flavor
1½ C. cold milk

¾ C. whipped topping
Blueberry or cherry pie filling

Prepare pudding as directed, only using 1½ C. milk. When pudding has set, top with fruit pie filling. If you want to, put this in a pie shell for a quick pie.

Peanut Butter Ice Cream

1 qt. vanilla ice cream
⅔ C. peanut butter

½ C. honey
½ C. chopped walnuts

Remove ice cream from freezer and let sit out for 10 to 20 minutes until somewhat softened. Press into loaf pan. Stir together peanut butter, honey, and peanuts. Swirl through ice cream and freeze for 4 to 6 hours or overnight. Serves 5 to 6.

Pineapple Ice Cream Pudding

2 env. unflavored gelatin
½ C. cold water
2 C. canned crushed pineapple
 and juice

½ C. sugar
1 qt. vanilla ice cream,
 slightly softened
 (leave out 10 to 20 minutes)

Sprinkle the gelatin over cold water to soften. Heat pineapple and sugar, stirring frequently until almost boiling and sugar is dissolved. Cool and chill until quite thick. Stir quickly into ice cream. Pour into mold and chill until firm. To unmold, wrap bottom of the mold with a warm wet towel. Rinse a plate with cold water to easier center the unmolded pudding.

Real Fudge Sauce (Cocoa)

1 (12 oz.) can evaporated milk
6 T. butter
½ C. plus 2 T. cocoa or
 3 (1 oz. ea.) squares

2 C. sugar
1½ tsp. vanilla

If using cocoa, make a paste with canned milk, carefully smoothing out lumps.

In a heavy saucepan, combine milk, butter, chocolate, and sugar. Over medium heat, bring the mixture to boil, stirring occasionally. Lower heat and stir constantly; cook 8 to 10 minutes. Remove from heat and stir in vanilla. Spoon warm (not hot) over vanilla ice cream. Use 1½ C. for topping on ice cream pie. Makes 2½ cups.

Rice is Nice Pudding

½ C. rice (not quick cooking)   4 C. milk
½ C. sugar   ½ C. raisins
¼ tsp. salt

Combine all ingredients in a large mixing bowl. Pour into buttered baking dish, cover, and bake 2 to 2½ hours. Remove the lid the last 15 minutes of baking time. Pudding will be creamy. This can be eaten plain or with a favorite sauce.

Snow Capped Pears

1 can pear halves (chilled)   Chocolate sauce
Whipped topping or   Candied cherries or
   whipped cream   red raspberries

Drain pear halves and place them cut-side up on a pretty plate, or individual serving plates. If necessary, cut a sliver off the rounded part of pear to level.

Top each pear half with whipped topping, drizzle with chocolate sauce, and top with a cherry.

Dressin' up is funner' than cookin'.

Chewy Fruit Leather

5 to 7 very ripe pears,   ⅓ C. sugar
   strawberries, plums or apricots

Peel and chop fruit to measure 5 cups. Put fruit and sugar in a heavy saucepan and bring mixture to a boil; stir to completely dissolve sugar. Puree in blender and cool. Cover cookie pan with plastic wrap and spread puree to 1/8-inch thickness.

Set pan on a level surface in the sunlight. Use a screen cover to avoid insects. Dry 20 to 24 hours. Bring sheet in at sunset and put out the next day. Fruit leather can be dried in a 150° oven with door open. When plastic peels off evenly, fruit is dry.

To store, place leather on a plastic sheet and roll up tightly. It will keep 3 to 4 weeks at room temperature; about 4 weeks in the refrigerator; about 1 year in the freezer.

To eat, just pull off chunks or slice into strips. Kids love this for an after-school treat.

Chocolate Tortoni

8 oz. semi-sweet chocolate
⅔ C. corn syrup, light or dark
2 C. heavy cream, divided

1½ C. broken crisp chocolate
  cookies
2 C. chopped walnuts, reserve 12
  halves for garnish

Place paper liners in 12 (2½-inch) muffin cups. Stir chocolate and corn syrup over very low heat until chocolate melts. Blend in ½ C. heavy cream and allow to cool.

Beat the remaining cream to softpeak stage; stir into chocolate mixture. Gently stir in cookies and nuts. Dip mixture into paper muffin cups.

Freeze 5 hours until firm. Let stand at room temperature a few minutes before serving. Serves 12.

Workin' out is funner than cookin'.

Main Dishes

Aurora Kielbasa Casserole

1½ C. cooked rice
1 can cream of mushroom soup
1 pkg. kielbasa (Polish sausage)
  (cut into small pieces)

1 C. shredded cheese or
  6 to 8 cheese slices

Put rice into a greased casserole using hands to break up the lumps. Add soup, sausage, and cheese. Bake at 350° for 20 to 25 minutes. Makes 5 to 6 servings. If you want to stretch this, stir in a package of frozen peas.

Baked Whole Chicken

1 baking chicken
½ lemon

1 stick butter, melted
Salt

Rub chicken inside and out with lemon; sprinkle with salt. If desired, fill loosely with stuffing. Rub melted butter over chicken and place on its side on baking rack. Place the rack in a roasting pan. Bake at 375° for 30 minutes, basting often. Turn bird to other side, bake, and baste another 30 minutes.

Turn breast side up. Baking time should be 25 to 30 minutes per pound. Continue basting until chicken is tender. Serves 7 to 8.

Beef and Bacon Patties, Broiled

1½ lbs. ground beef
4 T. chopped onion
1 clove garlic (minced)

1 T. Worcestershire sauce
8 slices bacon
(room temperature)

Place all ingredients except bacon in bowl and mix well. Shape mixture into 4 patties, place on baking sheet and put in freezer for 35 minutes. Remove from freezer.

Wrap 1 slice of bacon loosely around middle of each pattie; wrap a second slice the opposite direction around pattie, overlapping ends. Pierce the overlaps with a toothpick to secure.

Place in broiler 5 inches from heat for about 10 minutes or until nicely browned; turn patties and broil the other side. Serves 4.

Beef Pot Roast

3 to 5 lbs. beef roast
3 T. oil
1 large onion

2 garlic cloves
Salt

Trim most of the fat and discard. Heat oil very hot in Dutch oven or heavy pot with tight lid. Brown the meat to a dark rich color on all sides. Add sliced onion and garlic to the pan. Add ¾ C. boiling water, cover, and place in 325° oven. Cook for 2 to 3 hours or 25 to 30 minutes for each pound; 170° internal temperature.

Bridge Club Chicken Salad

1 (2 to 3 lb.) fryer
3 eggs, hard cooked and chopped
⅔ C. chopped celery

2 whole sweet pickles, chopped
¾ C. mayonnaise

Simmer cut-up fryer until tender. Drain, skin, and remove meat; chop into bite-size pieces. Combine all ingredients. Store covered in the refrigerator. Serve on lettuce leaves or use for sandwich filling.

Broiled Lamb Chops

6 lam chops, ¾ inch thick
Salt

3 T. melted butter

Preheat the broiler. Slash fat and coat lamb chops with melted butter. Place 3 inches from heat. Broil 4 minutes, turn and cook for 3 minutes longer. Sprinkle with salt. Serve with mint jelly.

Chicken Green Grape Salad

4 cooked, boned chicken breasts
2 C. green seedless grapes
Pimento strips

½ C. almonds, toasted
Mayonnaise

Chop chicken into bite-size pieces. Cut grapes in halves. Combine chicken, grapes, almonds, and enough mayonnaise to moisten; toss well. Can be served on lettuce leaves. Top each serving with 2 pimento strips. Serves 4.

Chicken N' Beef

1 pkg. dried beef
6 or 7 chicken breasts,
   skinned, split and boned

1 can mushroom soup
8 ozs. sour cream
Bacon slices

Line 9x13-inch pan or casserole with dried beef. Wrap raw bacon around the chicken pieces. Stir together soup and sour cream; pour over chicken. Cover with foil (or lid) and bake at 325° for 1¾ to 2 hours. Remove foil and let brown.

Chicken Livers Rosemary

1 lb. chicken livers
2 onions (sliced)
3 T. butter

½ tsp. rosemary (dried)
1/8 tsp. salt

Cut chicken livers in half and set aside. Separate onion slices into rings and saute' in skillet with butter until almost tender. Remove onions. Place chicken livers in skillet and stir-fry for 4 to 5 minutes. Add onions, rosemary, and salt. Cook and stir until liver is cooked through. Serves 3.

Billin' and Cooin' are funner than cookin'.

Chicken Fried Steak

2½ lbs. round steak
  (or cubed steak)
⅔ C. flour

Salt and pepper
⅓ C. oil

Trim and discard fat. Cut the meat into serving size pieces. Flour each piece and pound on both sides. Work as much flour into the meat as you can. If using cubed steak, simply flour well. Heat oil over high heat and brown steak on one side. Salt and pepper. Turn and season the other side. Let brown to a crisp rich brown. The juice makes delicious gravy.

Chowder Catfish Fillets

1 (10½ oz.) can frozen clam
  chowder (thawed)
½ C. milk
1 to 1½ lbs. catfish fillets

Lemon wedges
2 tsp. chopped fresh parsley

Combine chowder and milk in a small saucepan. Heat and stir until smooth. Arrange fillets in 1 layer in a casserole. Spoon soup over fish to completely cover. Bake at 350° for 10 to 15 minutes or until fish is cooked through. Garnish with parsley.

Cottage Omelets

1 can corned beef hash
2 T. oil

4 eggs
Salt and pepper

Divide the corned beef into 4 equal slices. Place oil in a skillet and brown hash lightly on both sides. Using a spoon, make an indentation in the center of each hash cake. Drop 1 egg into each indentation. Place lid on the skillet and cook over low heat until eggs are done. Season with salt and pepper. Serves 4.

Corned Beef Hash De Luxe

1 (15 oz.) can corned beef hash
Oil for frying

1 can cranberry-orange relish or
1 small can pineapple slices,
  drained

Slice corned beef hash into 1-inch slices. Pan fry to a golden brown. To serve, top each slice with cranberry-orange relish or a pineapple slice. Serves 4.

Fluffy Omelets

3 eggs, separated
1 C. cottage cheese,
  small curd

¼ tsp. vanilla
¼ C. flour
3 T. oil (for frying pan)

Beat egg whites until stiff. In a separate bowl beat yolks of eggs until lemon-colored; add cottage cheese, vanilla, and flour. Fold egg whites into this mixture. Cover surface of skillet with oil and drop 2 T. of batter for each omlet. Brown on both sides. Leftover ham or chicken can be added. Serves 4.

Crock Pot Chicken and Vegetables

1 fryer, cut-up
2 C. water
½ tsp. salt
4 carrots, cut chunk-size
3 small onions, peeled

If counting calories, chicken can be skinned before cooking. Place all ingredients in a slow-cooker. Cook on low heat for 4 to 5 hours until meat pulls away from the bones. Remove chicken and vegetables from the broth to a hot platter. This makes about 2½ cups of chopped chicken and 2 to 3 cups of broth.

Skatin' is funner than cookin'.

Crock Pot Duck

1 duck, cut-up
1 tsp. seasoned salt
3 carrots, cut-up

2 small onions, chopped
2 stalks celery, diced

Put 2 C. of water into crock pot and add all of the ingredients. Cook on high for 2½ hours. Remove and reserve vegetables as they become tender. Cook on low for 4 to 5 hours until duck is tender.

Crunchy Fried Fish

Fish, whatever you
    happen to catch

BATTER:
1 C. biscuit mix   ½ tsp. salt
1 egg   1 C. milk

Cut cleaned fish into serving-size pieces and pat dry. Make the batter, slowly stirring in the milk. Dip the fish in the batter and fry until golden brown.

Speedy Quiche

1 (9-inch) unbaked pastry shell   4 eggs, beaten
¾ C. cooked, diced ham   1½ C. milk
8 oz. Swiss cheese, shredded

Bake the pastry shell in 450° oven for 7 minutes. Remove from oven and turn heat to 325°. Cool the shell.

Stir together ham and cheese and pour into pie shell. Combine milk and eggs and pour over ham and cheese. Bake at 325° for 35 to 40 minutes. Custard should be firm. A knife inserted in the center will come out clean when quiche is done. Let stand 10 minutes before cutting. Serves 6.

Iowa Boy Pork Chops and Rice

6 thick pork chops
Cooking oil
1⅓ C. rice, uncooked

1 C. chicken bouillon
1 can chicken with rice soup

Fry pork chops in oil. Grease a 9x13-inch baking dish. Pour rice in dish, add bouillon and soup. Top with pork chops. Bake, covered at 350° over for 50 to 60 minutes. Uncover dish and bake another 10 to 12 minutes to brown chops.

Fish Diablo

1 lb. fish fillets
2 tsp. soy sauce
1 lemon

Garlic salt
Cayenne pepper

Clean fish and pat dry. Place on a large sheet of aluminum foil. Pull up edges of foil to form a "bowl". Combine soy sauce and juice from lemon. Pour over fish. Sprinkle with garlic salt and very lightly with cayenne pepper. Pull foil almost together, leaving a small opening for steam to escape. Place on a baking sheet. Bake at 350° for 15 to 20 minutes. Serves 2.

Fet's Onion Beef Pot Roast

3 to 5 lbs. boneless pot roast
1 envelope drdy onion soup mix
1 carrot, diced

Place the roast in the center of a large
sheet of aluminum foil. Sprinkle with
onion soup mix and carrot. Seal foil
with a double fold. Bake at 350° for
about 2 to 3 hours until tender. Be
careful to avoid steam when you un-
do the fold.

Fulton Frog Legs

8 frog legs
⅓ tsp. salt
1 lemon

1 egg, beaten
¾ C. cracker crumbs

Wash skinned frog legs in cold water; pat dry with paper towels. Salt lightly
and sprinkle with lemon juice. Dip legs in egg and cracker crumbs. Fry in
hot oil for 3 to 5 minutes.

Two tablespoons of reconstituted lemon juice equals the juice of one average-
size lemon. I just got a 32 oz. bottle of reconstituted lemon juice for 99 cents.
It's a lot less expensive and easier to use than fresh lemons. Freeze it in
ice cube trays and have it when you need it.

Germantown Hot Dogs and Kraut

3 Granny Smith apples,
  peeled and chopped
1 (27 oz.) can sauerkraut

3 T. brown sugar
1 tsp. caraway seeds
10 hot dogs

In kettle combine apples, sauerkraut with juice, brown sugar, and caraway seeds. Bring to boiling and simmer, covered for 20 minutes. Add hot dogs and simmer until heated. They're already cooked, so no need to boil hot dogs until they crack open.

Glazed Broiled Ham

1 lb. fully-cooked ham,
  center cut
2 T. apricot preserves

1 T. pineapple juice
½ tsp. Dijon-style mustard

Slash fat on edge of ham to prevent curling. Place on rack of broiler pan. Broil 3 inches from heat for 3 minutes. Turn and broil and additional 3 minutes. Combine preserves, pineapple juice, and mustard; spread over ham. Broil until glaze bubbles, about ½ to 1 minute.

Green Beans and Sausage Supper

1 lb. green beans
1 (12 oz.) pkg. link sausages

2 T. chopped onion

Clean and snap beans. Place in kettle and cover with water. Add onion and cut-up sausages. Cover and simmer until beans are barely tender. Serves 3 to 4.

Good Ol' Roast Beef

1 (3 to 4 lb.) chuck roast
2 medium onions, cut in pieces
4 C. water

¼ C. vinegar
3 T. soy sauce

Place all ingredients in a Dutch oven or roaster with lid. Cook in 325° oven for 3 to 4 hours or until meat is tender. Use cornstarch to thicken the juice for gravy.

Ham Loaf

1 lb. ground lean pork
1 lb. ground ham
14 small soda crackers,
  crushed

½ C. V-8 juice or
  tomato juice
2 eggs (beat yolks &
  whites separately)

Combine pork, ham, cracker crumbs, juice, and egg yolks. Fold in beaten egg whites. Bake at 350° for about 1½ hours. Serves 6 to 8.

Honeycomb Broiled Fish

4 to 5 fish fillets
2 T. olive oil

Honeycomb
Lemon wedges

Clean fillets and pat dry with paper towels. Rub the fish with olive oil and place on an oiled baking sheet. Broil for 6 to 7 minutes on each side. Remove from oven and put 2 teaspoons sliced honeycomb on each fillet. Turn broiler to high and broil fish to glaze the honeycomb. Honey will turn a light brown. Serve with lemon wedges.

Lemon Chicken

1 broiler-fryer chicken, cut-up
½ C. plus 1 T. lemon juice
Salt
Paprika

Place the pieces of chicken (not touching) in a shallow baking dish. Bake in preheated 375° for 15 minutes. Turn and bake another 15 minutes.

Remove from the oven and sprinkle with salt and paprika. Pour half of the lemon juice over chicken. Bake another 15 minutes. Turn again and sprinkle with remainder of lemon juice. Bake a few more minutes until juice runs clear.

Liver and Onions

1 to 1½ lbs. pork or beef liver
5 T. flour
3 T. bacon fat or oil

3 medium onions, sliced
Salt

Dredge liver with flour. Heat the bacon fat in skillet over moderate heat. Cook liver about 4 minutes, until browned, sprinkle with salt. turn, add sliced onions and salt lightly. Cover and cook until liver is done. Stir onions frequently; they should be crisp-tender. Serves 3 to 4.

Lobster Newberg

1 stick butter	2 T. sherry
1 T. flour	1 lb. well-drained
2 C. milk	cooked lobster

Melt butter in saucepan; add flour and stir to blend, but do not brown. Add milk, cook, and stir over low heat until thickened. Stir in sherry and lobster. Cook until heated through.

Meat Balls in An Instant

1 lb. ground beef	1 (10 oz.) can cream of
½ C. chopped onion	celery soup
1 (10 oz.) can golden	½ can water
mushroom soup	

Combine onion and ground beef; shape into balls. Fry until browned. Drain off fat; add soups and ½ can water. Stir and let simmer for 15 to 20 minutes. Serve over biscuits, toast or rice.

Orange Oven Chicken

1 fryer chicken, cut-up	¼ C. soy sauce
1½ C. orange soda	

Wash the chicken and dry with paper towels; sprinkle with salt and paprika and place in a foil-lined pan. Blend soda and soy sauce and pour over chicken. Bake at 350° for 45 minutes to 1 hour, basting occasionally.

Mississippi Meat Loaf Muffins

1½ lbs. hamburger
2 C. bread crumbs
1 (10 oz.) can condensed
 onion soup
8 stuffed olives
1 tsp. chopped parsley

Mix together all ingredients except olives. Distribute mixture into 12 (3-inch) muffin cups. Top each ''muffin'' with an olive. Bake at 400° for 15 to 20 minutes. Serves 6.

Orange Honey Glazed Ham

1 (3 lb.) canned ham
1 (3 oz.) pkg. orange
 gelatin

2 T. onion, chopped
1 tsp. ground cloves
1 T. honey

Drain ham; rub surface with cloves. Place ham on a large sheet of heavy-duty aluminum foil. Place on rack in baking pan. Sprinkle dry gelatin over ham and drizzle with honey. Close foil with ''grocery store'' fold. Bake at 350° for 1 hour. Open foil, being careful to avoid steam, and bake another 30 minutes. Serves 8 to 10.

Oven Pork Chops

6 Iowa pork chops
3 T. brown sugar
10 onion slices

¾ C. chili sauce or catsup
6 lemon slices

Arrange chops in a single layer in baking pan. Sprinkle with brown sugar. Divide the onion slices into rings and place on top of brown sugar. Top with chili sauce (or catsup) and lemon slices. Add enough water to come half-way up on the pork chops. Bake, uncovered in 350° for 2½ hours. Uncover and bake another 30 minutes.

Pork Chops Crisp

4 pork chops
2 eggs, beaten
Whole soda crackers

Salt
½ C. oil

Place crackers in a large plastic bag and close. Roll with a rolling pin to make crumbs. Beat eggs, dip pork chops in egg mixture, then in cracker crumbs. Fry in hot oil until very brown; sprinkle with salt. Turn chops and repeat process.

Quick Shrimp Newburg

1 (10½ oz.) can Newburg sauce
1 C. cooked shrimp, drained

2 eggs, hard cooked

Empty Newburg sauce into saucepan. Add shrimp and chopped eggs. Cook and stir until heated through. I like to serve this on hot biscuits or toast.

Real Good Catfish

Catfish, or any other fish
1 can cream of vegetable soup

Soup can of milk
Butter to grease pan

Place serving size pieces of fish in a greased baking dish. Stir together the milk and soup; pour over fish. Bake at 350° for 25 to 30 minutes or until fish flakes.

Rock River Rice

3 slices crisp-cooked bacon,
  crumbled (reserve grease)
½ C. chopped onion

¼ C. chopped green pepper
1¾ C. spaghetti sauce (Prego)
3 C. cooked rice

Cook onion and green pepper in bacon grease. Add the spaghetti sauce and rice. Heat through and sprinkle top with the crumbled bacon. Serves 6.

Salmon Celery Loaf

1 (1 lb.) can salmon & juice
1½ C. cracker crumbs
½ C. chopped green pepper
2 eggs, beaten
1 can cream of celery soup

Combine all ingredients in bowl. Pat mixture into greased loaf pan. Bake for 50 to 60 minutes at 350°. Delicious served with tartar sauce.

Shawneetown Short Ribs

5 lbs. short ribs
½ C. flour
2 T. oil

½ tsp. salt
1 large onion (chopped)

Dredge ribs with flour; brown in oil in Dutch oven. Sprinkle with salt and add onion. Cover and simmer for 1½ to 2½ hours until meat is tender. Add just a little water if necessary.

Hot Cheddar Chicken

1 fryer, cut-up
Taco sauce, medium hot
2 C. sharp Cheddar cheese, shredded

Tortilla chips, broken
1 T. parsley, chopped

Pour taco sauce over chicken in greased casserole. Cover and bake at 350° for 1¼ to 1½ hours. Sprinkle cheese over the chicken and top with tortilla chips. Bake, uncovered until cheese melts. Garnish with chopped parsley.

Spiced Ham Supreme

5 to 7 lb. fully cooked ham
1 C. brown sugar
1 C. apple juice

1 C. bouillon, chicken flavored
1 tsp. ground cloves

Pierce ham all over with sharp fork; place in a heavy plastic bag. Combine all ingredients and pour over ham in the bag; close. Marinate for 24 hours or longer, turning occasionally.

Drain ham and bake for 2 to 2½ hours. Internal temperature should be 140°.

If using uncooked ham, bake 2½ to 3 hours. Internal temperature should be 160°.

Surprise Eggs and Sausage

6 hard-cooked eggs
2 eggs (beaten)
1 lb. loose, spicy sausage meat

1 C. bread crumbs
Oil for frying

Beat the 2 eggs and mix ½ of the mixture with the meat. Peel the hard-cooked eggs and spread sausage evenly all around the outside of the eggs. Dip the sausage-covered eggs in the remaining egg to coat, then roll in the bread crumbs. Fry in hot oil, rolling them as they cook. Drain on paper towels, cool, and chill. Great for breakfast or supper.

Uncle George's
Corned Beef in Beer

6 potatoes, peeled & quartered
3 medium onions, quartered

1½ C. thinly sliced carrots
3 to 4 lbs. corned beef
1 C. beer

Place vegetables in bottom of crock pot; turn on low heat. Trim excess fat from meat and place on top of vegetables; add beer. Cook 9½ to 11 hours or until meat is tender. Save the broth for some tasty vegetable soup.

(106)

Wildwood Venison

Venison   Salt
Flour   Oil for frying
1 to 2 C. cream or more
  to cover meat

Cut venison into stew-size pieces. Dredge with flour and brown in oil in Dutch oven. Pour in cream, cover, and simmer over LOW heat until meat is tender.

If you want to make gravy, add enough water to the juice to make 1½ cups. Boil to dissolve ''crispies'' in the cooking pan. Add 4 spoons of flour to ½ C. water in a jar with a lid and shake well. Add to juices; cook and stir for 2 to 3 minutes. Season with salt and pepper.

Spoonin' is funner' than cookin'.

(107)

Cheddar Sausage Rolls

16 sausage links   1 ¼ C. shredded Cheddar cheese
16 thin slices white bread   ¼ C. butter

Cook sausage until done and drain on paper towels. Cut crusts from bread. Combine cheese and butter and spread on both sides of the bread. Roll a sausage in each slice and secure with toothpicks. Place on oiled baking pan and bake at 400° for 10 to 12 minutes.

Roast Tenderloin of Beef

1 beef tenderloin, 4 to 6 lbs.   ½ tsp. fresh dill
1 clove garlic, halved

Rub meat all over with cut side of garlic; place on rack in roasting pan. Place tapered end under. Roast in 450° oven for 45 to 60 minutes. For rare beef, cook to 140° on meat thermometer. To serve, cut into thin slices and garnish with fresh dill.

Pies and Pastries

Apple Cinnamon Pie

6 to 8 large apples,
  peeled & sliced*
1 to 1½ C. sugar
2 T. flour

¾ tsp. cinnamon
Unbaked pastry for 2-crust pie

Combine sugar, flour, and cinnamon and stir in with apples. Fill bottom crust with mixture. Top with crust and cut slits so steam can escape. Bake at 400° for 50 to 60 minutes. Check to be sure apples are done.

*Two (1 lb. 4 oz.) cans of sliced pie apples can be used instead of fresh apples.

Banana Cream Pie

1 (3½ oz.) pkg. instant banana or
  vanilla pudding mix
2 C. milk

2 large bananas, sliced
1 prepared pie shell, baked
Whipped cream or
  whipped topping

Prepare the pudding as directed on the package. Slice the bananas into the baked pie shell. Pour the pudding over the bananas; refrigerate. Just before serving top with whipped cream.

(109)

Butter Pecan Ice Cream Pie

3 C. butter pecan ice cream
1 C. milk
1 (3 3/8 oz.) pkg. instant
  butterscotch pudding

1 baked 8-inch pie shell
  (or graham cracker crust)

Stir together softened ice cream and milk. Add pudding mix and beat for about 1 minute. Pour into pie shell and refrigerate 1 to 2 hours before serving.

Cherry Ice Cream Pie

1 (3 oz.) pkg. cherry gelatin
1½ C. boiling water
1 C. sweet cherries (drained)

2 C. (1 pt.) cherry ice cream
  (cut into pieces)
1 (8-inch) graham cracker crust

Dissolve gelatin in the water; add cherries and ice cream. When cool, chill until it begins to thicken. Stir and pour into the pie shell. Allow to chill until the gelatin is firm.

Classic Fruit Cobbler

½ C. margarine
1 C. biscuit mix
¾ C. sugar
1 C. milk

4 C. fruit, drained
(cherries, blackberries, peaches
or any combination)

Melt margarine in 10x6-inch baking dish. Add biscuit mix, sugar, and milk. Stir to blend. Top with fruit. If unsweetened cherries are used, increase sugar ⅓ to ½ cup. Bake at 375° for 30 to 40 minutes. Top should be a light golden brown. Good topped with whipped cream or ice cream. Serves 5 to 6.

Classic Poke Cake

1 pkg. yellow cake mix
3¼ C. water (1¼ C. for cake)
 2 C. for gelatin

⅓ C. vegetable oil
3 eggs
1 box strawberry gelatin

Prepare cake mix according to directions on the box and bake in greased 13x9-inch pan. Cool cake in pan for 20 minutes.

Prepare gelatin by dissolving in 1 cup of boiling water. Stir in one cup of ice water. Use a fork to pierce holes in every inch of top of cake. Pour gelatin evenly over cooled cake. Chill at least 2 hours in the refrigerator. Looks festive decorated with whipped cream.

Coffee Ice Cream Pie

1 (9-inch) Keebler chocolate
   pie crust
1 qt. coffee ice cream
1½ C. chilled fudge sauce
1 C. chopped nuts

Fill crust with softened ice cream and freeze until very firm. Spread fudge sauce over the top and sprinkle with nuts. Freeze overnight.

Cookie Pie Crust

1½ C. crushed cookie crumbs or
   graham cracker crumbs
5 T. margarine, melted
3 T. confectioner's sugar
1 tsp. flour

Place all ingredients in bowl and mix well. Press into a 9-inch pie tin. Bake at 350° for 6 to 10 minutes. Cool before filling.

Never Fail No Bake Pie Crust

½ C. butter, melted
1½ C. granola

½ C. chopped nuts
3 T. brown sugar

Combine all ingredients and stir well. Press in an 8-inch pie pan. Refrigerate until firm.

Deep River Fried Pies

1 (8 oz.) pkg. mixed dried fruit
1¾ C. water
½ C. sugar

2 (9-inch) prepared pie crusts,
room temperature
Oil for deep frying

Combine fruit and water in a heavy saucepan. Cook over low heat for 15 minutes. Add sugar and cook another 20 minutes over very low heat. Stir frequently to prevent scorching. Fruit should be thickened and quite dry. If it isn't, cook a little longer. Set aside to cool.

Place 1 pie crust on lightly floured board. Rub rolling pin with flour and roll crust flat. Cut into rounds (about 4 inches) and place a tablespoon of filling in center of each round. Moisten edges with water, fold over and press edges together. Seal with tines of a fork.

Heat oil to 375°. Fry pies 4 to 5 minutes, turn and fry another 3 to 4 minutes. Drain on paper towels. Makes 12 to 14 pies.

Fruit Yogurt Pie

6 ozs. strawberry yogurt
3½ C. thawed whipped topping
½ C. chopped strawberries

6 ozs. blueberry yogurt
1 graham cracker crust

Measure 1¾ C. whipped topping and fold into strawberries. Smooth over bottom of crust. Fold remainder of topping with blueberry yogurt. Spoon over first layer. Freeze for 5 hours. Place in refrigerator for about 1 hour before serving. Freeze leftover pie.

Kahlua Ice Cream Pie

1 pt. chocolate ice cream
1 (9-inch) Keebler chocolate
  crust

2 T. Kahlua liquer
3½ C. vanilla ice cream
½ C. nuts, chopped

Have ice creams at room temperature, but not melted. Smooth chocolate ice cream over bottom of crust. Using a teaspoon, spread Kahlua over chocolate ice cream. Pile on vanilla ice cream. Sprinkle top with chopped nuts. Freeze until serving time.

Mom's Rhubarb Pie

4 C. rhubarb, cut in
  1-inch pieces
1½ C. sugar
6 T. flour

3 T. butter
Pastry for 2-crust pie

Stir together sugar and flour. Sprinkle 4 T. over crust in pan. Sprinkle remaining sugar-flour mixture over rhubarb and stir quickly to coat it. Pour into pie crust and dot with butter. Moisten edge of bottom water. Adjust top crust, press, and trim. Make a few slits in the top so steam can escape.

Mom used to sprinkle a little sugar on the top crust, which makes it brown nicely. Bake at 450° for 15 minutes, turn heat to 350° and bake another 45 minutes.

(To soften ice cream for pie, leave out of the freezer for 10 to 20 minutes.)

No Crust Nut Cracker Pie

24 round, rich, butterflavored
   crackers, crushed (about 1 C.)
3 egg whites

1 C. sugar
2 tsp. baking powder
1 C. nuts, chopped or ground

Beat egg whites, add sugar and baking powder to make meringue. Fold in cracker crumbs and nuts. Pour into greased pie pan. Bake at 350° for 25 to 30 minutes until lightly browned and knife in center comes out clean.

(I often drizzle this with fudge sauce before serving.)

Old Niota Mincemeat Pie

1 jar (32 oz.) prepared mincemeat
½ tsp. grated orange peel
1 apple, finely chopped

2 unbaked prepared pie crusts
Milk

Combine all ingredients and pour into pie shell. Moisten edges of crust and cover with top crust. Press edges together to seal and trim off excess crust. Rub surface of the crust with milk. Cut slits so steam can escape. Bake at 425° for 10 minutes. Lower heat to 350° and bake another 45 minutes.

Ken's Whole Wheat Pie Crust

1 C. whole-wheat flour
1 C. white flour
7 T. margarine

¼ tsp. salt
4 T. ice water

Work margarine into flour with hands or pastry blender until it looks like coarse cornmeal. Add water and stir with fork to blend. Shape into a ball and refrigerate for 20 minutes.

On a floured surface, roll dough slightly larger than your pie pan. This dough breaks easily. When this happens, simply press it back together again. The delicious nutty flavor is worth the effort. Pierce with fork and bake at 375° for 7 to 10 minutes for 1-crust cream pie.

Blueberry Pie

1 pie crust, frozen
1 (No. 2) can blueberry pie
  filling

1/8 tsp. cinnamon
Whipped topping

Pierce room temperature pie crust all over with sharp fork. Bake at 450° for 10 minutes. When cool, pour in pie filling. Sprinkle with cinnamon and smooth on whipped topping.

Temptation Pie

3 to 4 ripe bananas
1 baked pie crust

Whipped topping
Chocolate curls

Slice bananas to fill pie crust. Pile on whipped topping and garnish with chocolate curls.

Pie Crust

2 C. flour
½ tsp. salt

⅔ C. shortening
⅓ C. ice water

Sift the flour and salt; cut in the shortening until no pieces are larger than peas. Sprinkle on the water, 1 T. at a time, and toss with a fork. Add just enough water to hold the dough together so it can be handled and rolled out. This makes one 2-crust pie.

To get a beautiful brown top crust, brush top with milk before baking.

Pralines and Cream Pie

1 prepared 9-inch chocolate
   pie shell
1 qt. pralines & cream ice cream

1½ C. chilled fudge sauce
½ C. pecans, chopped

Fill crust with softened ice cream. Freeze until firm. Spread fudge sauce over ice cream; sprinkle with nuts and freeze overnight. This a great fix-ahead dessert, and so delicious.

(117)

Rum Ice Cream Pie

5 T. peanut butter

½ C. light brown sugar, packed

2 T. light rum

1 qt. vanilla ice cream, slightly softened, not melted

Chocolate or graham cracker crust

Melt the peanut butter and brown sugar in a heavy skillet over very low heat. Remove from the heat and stir in rum. When cool, stir with softened ice cream. Pour into the crust and freeze until firm. I sometimes sprinkle chopped peanuts over this.

Sour Cream Pie Topping

1 C. sour cream

2 T. brown sugar

2 T. lemon juice

Optional: ¼ C. nuts

Stir together cream, sugar, and lemon juice. If using on pumpkin pie, let pie cool for 20 minutes. Top with sour cream mixture and sprinkle with nuts. Place in 350° and bake for 10 minutes. This is delicious on any pie made with cooked pudding.

Readin' is funner than cookin'.

Salads, Dressings and Vinegars

Anne's Low Calorie Salad Dressing

½ C. wine vinegar
1/8 tsp. salt

2 T. apple juice concentrate
¾ C. water

Shake in a pint jar. Store in the refrigerator. Makes 1⅓ cups.

Apricot Pineapple Mold

1 (6 oz.) pkg. orange gelatin
1 (20 oz.) can crushed pineapple

2 (30 oz. ea.) cans apricots

Drain fruit, reserving juice. Add water to juice to make 3 cups. Bring juice to a boil and add gelatin, stirring to dissolve. In bowl stir together chopped apricots, pineapple and sour cream. Stir into gelatin mixture and pour into mold. Top with any fruit salad dressing. Serves 12.

Dinin' out is funner than cookin'.

(119)

Adel's Dill Vinegar

Fresh dill weed   2 C. cider vinegar

Fill a pint mason jar with leaves and stems of dill. Fill the jar with vinegar, covering the dill. Place outside in the sun and let stand for 2 weeks. Strain through a strainer with fine mesh. Use for making salad dressings. Makes about 1½ cups.

Asparagus Olive Salad

3 (10 oz. ea.) pkgs. frozen   4 to 5 stuffed olives for
  asparagus   garnish
1 (8 oz.) bottle Italian dressing

Cook asparagus until tender; drain. Cover with Italian dressing and refrigerate. Turn spears occasionally. Garnish with sliced olives.

Asparagus 'N Egg Salad

2 (15 oz. ea.) cans asparagus   2 hard-cooked eggs
Vinaigrette salad dressing   Pimiento strips

Drain the asparagus. (I always put the juice in my soup jar in the freezer.) Toss the asparagus with the vinaigrette dressing and chill.

When ready to serve, garnish with eggs and pimiento strips. Serves 4 to 6.

Avocado with Shrimp

3 avocados
2½ C. cleaned shrimp,
  chilled

Spinach or lettuce leaves
Cherry tomatoes, halved
Mayonnaise

Clean avocados and cut in half lengthwise; cut-up tomatoes. Fill each avocado half with shrimp and tomatoes. Serve on a lettuce leaf and top with mayonnaise. Serves 6.

Carrot Coleslaw

2 C. shredded cabbage
½ C. shredded carrot
1 T. minced onion

1/8 tsp. salt
⅓ C. mayonnaise

In bowl combine cabbage, carrot, and onion. Sprinkle with salt. Add mayonnaise and toss. Cover and refrigerate. Toss again just before serving. Serves 4.

Carrot Salad, Congealed

1 pkg. lemon or orange gelatin
1 (8 oz.) can crushed pineapple
1½ C. grated carrots

½ C. nuts, chopped
Optional: 1 T. chopped
  green pepper

Drain pineapple pressing out as much juice as possible. Add water to juice to make 2 C. of liquid. Dip out and discard 1 T. of liquid. Heat liquid to boiling; add gelatin and stir to dissolve. Chill until starting to congeal. Stir in pineapple, carrots, nuts, and green pepper if using. Pour into 1½-quart mold. Chill until firm.

Citrus Dressing

4 T. fresh lemon juice
2 T. fresh orange juice
1 T. honey

1 T. olive oil
1½ tsp. grated orange peel

Combine all ingredients and refrigerate. Use on fruit salads or greens. Shake before using.

Citrus Onion Salad

6 navel oranges
1 onion

¾ C. black olives,
chopped

Peel and slice oranges. Slice onion very thin and separate rings. Combine all ingredients. Serve with or without dressing. Serves 6.

Coleslaw Dressing

½ C. whipping cream
2 T. plus 2 tsp. vinegar

½ tsp. sugar
¼ tsp. salt

Beat cream until not quite stiff. Slowly add remaining ingredients and beat until it will hold peaks.

Egg Salad

6 eggs, hard-cooked & chopped
2 T. minced onion
2 T. sweet pickle, minced or
    pickle relish

2 tsp. pickle juice
4 T. mayonnaise

Combine all ingredients and chill for 3 to 4 hours. This salad can be used for sandwiches or served in lettuce cups. Makes about 1½ cups.

Garden Tomato Salad

6 tomatoes, unpeeled & chopped
1 red onion, sliced
2 small cucumbers, thinly sliced

6 spinach leaves
¼ C. Italian dressing

Toss all ingredients together. Refrigerate until ready to use. Makes 6 servings.

(123)

Garlic Flavored Oil

1½ C. peanut (or other) oil
6 to 8 cloves garlic

Clean and peel garlic, place on chopped board and smash with side of
cleaver. Pour oil and garlic into a pint
jar with a tight lid.

Garlic flavored oil is excellent for stir-
frying and can be used in any recipe
that calls for minced garlic. This will
keep 3 to 4 weeks in the refrigerator.

Swingin' is funner than cookin'.

Greek Salad Dressing

½ C. olive oil
5 T. white vinegar
½ tsp. garlic salt

1 T. minced onion
1 T. green pepper, minced

Combine all ingredients in shaker bottle. I don't care what anyone else does,
I store all my salad dressings in the refrigerator.

Green Sleeves Yogurt Dressing

1 C. plain yogurt
3 T. chopped parsley, fresh
Salt

¼ C. chopped spinach
½ tsp. dried dill

Blend in food processor. Refrigerate until used. Serve on salad or use as
dip for raw vegetables.

(124)

Ham Salad

1 C. ground cooked ham
3 T. chopped celery
2 T. pickle relish, drained

½ tsp. horseradish
4 T. mayonnaise

Toss all ingredients together. Delicious on lettuce and tomato or as a sandwich filling.

Mandarin Cottage Cheese Salad

2 C. cottage cheese
1 C. crushed pineapple, drained
1 can mandarin oranges, drained

2 C. whipped topping
1 (3 oz.) pkg. orange gelatin, (use dry)

Stir together cottage cheese, pineapple, oranges, and whipped topping. Sprinkle dry gelatin over this and stir. Chill for several hours. Serve on lettuce or spinach leaves.

Instant Fruit Salad Dressing or Dip

1 box instant vanilla
   pudding mix
2½ C. light cream

1 T. sugar
1 tsp. vanilla

Combine all ingredients in mixing bowl and beat at low speed for 2 minutes. Cover with plastic wrap and refrigerate for 3 hours or overnight. Makes 2½ cups.

(125)

Lemon Dressing

½ C. sour cream
½ C. mayonnaise
4 T. lemon juice

½ tsp. salt
2 T. chives, chopped

Combine all ingredients. Very good on green salads.

*Picnickin' is funner
than cookin'.*

Mint Jade Dressing

4 T. white wine vinegar
1 T. vegetable oil

2 T. chopped fresh mint leaves
1 tsp. sugar

Combine all ingredients. Shake before serving. Good on both vegetable and fruit salads.

Papaya Salad

4 C. salad greens, torn into
   bite-size pieces
2 C. cooked shrimp

½ C. French dressing
2 papayas, cut into fourths

Salad greens should be crisp and dry. Marinate shrimp in French dressing for 2 to 3 hours. Arrange lettuce on salad plates. Top with 2 slices papaya. Garnish with shrimp. Serves 4.

Peach Pineapple Frozen Salad

1 (20 oz.) can crushed pineapple, drained
1 can peach pie filling
1 T. chopped maraschino cherries

1 can Eagle Brand milk
1 (12 oz.) carton whipped topping

Combine all ingredients and pour into 9x13x2-inch pan; freeze.

Potato Salad

6 potatoes
3 T. chopped onion
3 hard-cooked eggs, chopped

Salt
1 C. mayonnaise (or more)

Peel and dice potatoes; boil for about 10 minutes or until tender. Drain and sprinkle potatoes, eggs, and onions lightly with salt. Toss with mayonnaise and chill.

When I open a can of green beans or peas, I always freeze the juice to use when boiling potatoes for salad. It makes the salad zesty and adds extra vitamins.

Red Apple Cole Slaw

1½ C. unpeeled, diced red apple
2 C. cabbage, finely shredded
¼ C. seedless raisins

½ C. chopped nuts
½ C. coleslaw dressing

Combine all ingredients and toss well to distribute dressing. Chill if not using right away.

Red Fox Bean Salad

1 (30 oz.) can red kidney beans
2 hard-cooked eggs, chopped
4 T. chopped onion

4 T. chopped sweet pickles
⅓ C. mayonnaise (or more)

Drain kidney beans. Combine all ingredients and toss lightly to mix. Refrigerate covered. Serves 4.

Snow Pea 'N Chicken Salad

1½ C. snow peas, cut bite-size
¾ C. red bell pepper strips, halved

¼ onion, sliced
1 C. cooked chicken, chopped

Clean, trim, and blanch snow peas. Drain and pat dry. Combine all ingredients in a bowl. Refrigerate for an hour or more. Serve on lettuce leaves with your favorite dressing. Serves 4 to 5.

Sour Cream Salad Dressing

½ C. (4 oz.) sour cream
2 T. vinegar

½ tsp. salt
1 tsp. sugar

Combine all ingredients and stir to dissolve the sugar. If the vinegar is very strong, adjust the sugar to taste. Use on or in both fruit and vegetables salads.

Popeye Salad

1 lb. spinach, torn into
  bite-size pieces
3 tomatoes, chopped

1 C. sliced mushrooms
½ C. onion rings
Vinaigrette dressing

Combine ingredients. Toss with dressing to coat leaves. Serves 6 to 7.

Tarragon Vinegar

Fresh Tarragon

2 C. cider vinegar

Fill a pint jar with leaves and stalks of tarragon. Then fill the jar with vinegar, covering the leaves. Place outside in the sun and let stand for 2 to 3 weeks. Strain through a strainer with fine mesh.

Use to flavor sharp sauces, or when making mayonnaise or French dressing.

Makes about 1½ cups.

Flirtin' is funner than cookin'.

Tuna Salad in a Minute

1 (6½ oz.) can water-packed   ¼ C. chopped onion
   tuna, drained   Salt
⅓ C. chopped celery   Mayonnaise

Combine all ingredients. Store covered in the refrigerator. Serve on lettuce leaves or use for sandwich filling.

Vinaigrette Dressing

½ C. salad oil   1/8 tsp. salt
2 T. vinegar   Pepper
1½ tsp. sugar

Combine all ingredients in a jar. Shake until the sugar is dissolved. You may want to add a little more sugar. Store in the refrigerator. Use this on cooked vegetable salads, too. Makes ½ cup.

Orange Sour Cream Salad

1 (8½ oz.) can fruit cocktail   1 C. (8 oz.) sour cream
1 (11 oz.) can mandarin oranges   ½ C. nuts, chopped
Large box orange gelatin

Drain juice from fruit cocktail and oranges. Add enough water to make 2 cups. Bring 1 cup of mixture to boiling, add gelatin and stir to dissolve. Stir in additional cup of juice and refrigerate. Combine fruit, sour cream, and nuts. When gelatin is consistency of egg white; fold in sour cream mixture; refrigerate. Serve with fruit salad dressing.

Veggies

Ace's Carmelized Whole Sweet Onions

1½ lbs. small onions
½ stick margarine
1½ tsp. sugar

Salt
Optional: red bell pepper
   strips

Peel onions; cut cross on bottom of each one to prevent separation. Bring salted water to boiling. Add onions and simmer covered for 25 minutes. Drain and rinse with cold water. Pat dry on paper towels. Heat margarine in heavy skillet. When margarine foams add onions. When heated through, sprinkle with salt and sugar. Shake the skillet until onions are coated. Cook until onions turn a rich brown.

Anise Carrots

1 tsp. butter
4 C. thinly sliced carrots
3 T. water
¼ tsp. anise seeds, crushed
Salt

Melt butter in skillet; add all ingredients. Stir-fry until carrots are coated.

Cover and cook until crisp-tender. It may be necessary to add water.

Check frequently as carrots burn easily.

Banker's Eggplant

1 large or 2 medium eggplants
French dressing
1 or 2 cloves garlic

Sour cream
Chives or green onions
with tops

Smash garlic and place in jar with French dressing. Peel eggplants and slice into ¾-inch slices. Marinated for 1 hour in French dressing.

Bake at 450° for 25 minutes. Remove eggplant from oven and spread with sour-cream chive mixture. With oven door open, heat an additional 5 minutes.

Broccoli and Cashews

1 (10 oz.) pkg. frozen
  broccoli spears
½ C. whole cashews

1 T. butter
2 tsp. finely shredded
  lemon peel

Cook broccoli and drain well. Heat butter in small heavy skillet; add cashews, cook and stir for 2 minutes or until lightly browned. Remove from heat and stir in lemon rind. Put broccoli in a pretty serving dish and top with cashews. Serves 4.

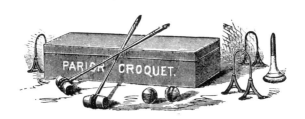

Croquet is funner' than cookin'.

Broccoli Sesame

4 C. broccoli florets
4 tsp. toasted sesame seeds
¾ tsp. sesame seed oil

1½ T. lemon juice
Optional: Chopped red bell pepper
for garnish

Simmer broccoli until crisp-tender; drain. Stir together remaining ingredients. Pour over broccoli and garnish with chopped red bell pepper, if desired.

Butter Beans

2⅔ C. dried butter beans or
lima beans
3 qts. water

½ C. chopped onion
1 tsp. salt
6 strips bacon or ham hocks

Soak beans in water overnight. Or, bring to a boil, simmer 3 minutes, and let stand for 1 hour. Rinse, cover with water; add onion and bacon (or ham hocks). Simmer, uncovered for about 30 to 40 minutes until beans are tender. Add salt and simmer another 4 to 5 minutes.

Crock Pot Corn

½ stick butter or margarine
4 T. water

2 T. sugar
20 ozs. frozen corn

Cook in crock pot on Low for 3½ to 4 hours.

(133)

Better Brussel Sprouts

3 T. butter or margarine
⅔ C. chicken broth or bouillon
1 onion, chopped

2 pkgs. frozen brussel sprouts
½ tsp. salt

Place butter and chicken broth or bouillon in saucepan. Bring to a boil and add brussel sprouts. Reduce heat, cover and cook 10 to 15 minutes until just tender. Optional: Place drained brussel sprouts in oven-proof dish. Top with 1 cup shredded Cheddar cheese and broil until cheese has melted.

Cabbage in Cream

1 medium head cabbage
3 T. butter
1 C. whipping cream

Salt
Optional: a light sprinkling
  of nutmeg

Peel off tough or yellowed outer leaves. Slice cabbage in half, then into fourths. Shred coarsely, wash well and drain. Cook cabbage in boiling salt water for 4 minutes. Remove from heat and drain, squeezing out as much water as possible.

Melt butter in Dutch oven or heavy saucepan. Add cabbage, cream, and salt. Simmer, covered over very low heat for 5 to 10 minutes, stirring often. Dust with nutmeg, if desired.

Cauliflower with Cheese Sauce

1 cauliflower
⅓ C. mayonnaise
2 tsp. prepared mustard

2 C. Cheddar cheese, shredded
2 T. chopped parsley

Cook cauliflower in boiling water until tender; drain well. Spread cauliflower with combined mayonnaise and mustard. Top with cheese. Place in 350° oven for 10 minutes or until cheese melts. Serves 6 to 8.

Dilly Zucchini

2 medium zucchini
3 T. butter
Dill weed, fresh or dried

Optional: red bell pepper strips
    to garnish

Cut 2 unpeeled zucchini in half lengthwise. Cook, covered in boiling salted water for 12 to 15 minutes or until tender. Drain, brush with melted butter, sprinkle with dill weed, and bell pepper, if using. If you don't have bell pepper, a sprinkle of paprika will add some color.

Dreamland Sweet Potatoes

6 sweet potatoes
1½ sticks butter
1½ C. sugar

¾ C. orange juice
¾ C. pecans, chopped

Boil sweet potatoes until tender. Peel and mash; add all ingredients. Pour in 2-quart casserole and bake at 350° until well heated. Optional: If you like a really sweet dish, this can be topped with miniature marshmallows. Bake until browned.

Fried Squash Parmesan

6 small squash
1 C. cornmeal
¼ tsp. salt

¾ C. cooking oil
Parmesan cheese, grated

Slice squash ¼-inch thick. Stir cornmeal and salt together and coat squash with mixture. Saute' squash slices until brown; turn and sprinkle with Parmesan cheese. Cook until browned and tender. Serves 6.

Green Beans in Sour Cream Sauce

3 C. green beans
½ C. liquid from green beans
1 pkg. French's sour cream
   & chives mix
½ C. milk
Optional: ½ C. slivered almonds or
   red bell pepper strips for garnish

Cook green beans without salt; drain, reserving ½ C. green bean liquid and ½ C. milk in saucepan. Cook and stir over low heat until sauce thickens.

Bowlin' is funner than cookin'.

Green Peas with Walnuts

2 boxes frozen green beans   ½ C. walnuts
½ stick margarine   1/8 tsp. salt
1 can mushrooms, drained & chopped

Melt margarine in skillet. Saute' peas, mushrooms, and walnuts 6 to 8 minutes until peas are done. Sprinkle with salt. Serves 6.

Grilled Tomatoes

6 firm tomatoes   Dried basil or curry powder
4 T. butter, melted   Salt

Cut tomatoes in half crosswise. Place in greased baking dish. Brush with melted butter and season with salt. Sprinkle lightly with basil or curry powder or a combination of both. Place about 6 inches from broiler heat. Tomatoes should cook slowly. Do not turn. Place in aluminum foil to cook on grill. It will take 10 to 12 minutes.

Farmer Brown Carrots

2½ C. sliced raw carrots   3 eggs, beaten
½ C. butter   2 C. grated Cheddar cheese
½ C. milk

Boil carrots until tender. Mash, add butter, milk, and eggs. Fold in Cheddar cheese. Bake at 350° for 40 to 50 minutes.

Hassleback Potatoes

6 potatoes (small enough to fit
   in large, deep spoon)
¼ C. melted butter

2 T. dry bread crumbs
4 T. grated Parmesan cheese
Salt

Peel potatoes and put in cold water. Place a potato in a large deep spoon. Make ⅓-inch vertical slices to the spoon which will keep the knife from cutting through the potato. Place potato in cold water. Finish slicing potatoes. Drain potatoes and pat dry.

Place potatoes cut-side up in buttered casserole. Brush them with melted butter and sprinkle with salt. Bake at 425° basting occasionally for 25 minutes.

Remove from oven and sprinkle with bread crumbs; bake another 15 minutes.

Sprinkle with Parmesan cheese and bake for 5 more minutes.

YES, THEY ARE WORTH THE HASSLE!

Hasslin' is funner' than cookin'.

Illini Kale Supreme

2 lbs. kale
3 T. butter
Salt

1 C. plain yogurt
Optional: Sprinkle of nutmeg

Wash kale several times: remove thick stems. Place kale on chopping board and chop finely. Add to saucepan containing boiling salted water. Cover and simmer for 15 to 20 minutes. Drain in collander and return kale to saucepan. Add butter and salt. Heat over very low heat. Add yogurt and heat through but do not boil. Serves 3 to 4.

If you're not a kale user, PLEASE put out at least 3 plants to try it. You can cut leaves and the plant keeps right on growing, it's super for stir-fry cooking, highly nutritious, and tolerates drought. It makes an attractive garnish, too.

Jessie's Mashed Sweet Potato Casserole

4 medium sweet potatoes,
　to make 3 C. mashed
2 T. molasses

3 T. butter
Optional: Chopped parsley to
　garnish

Pour mashed sweet potatoes into buttered casserole. Heat molasses and butter in a small saucepan; pour over sweet potatoes. Bake at 350° for 30 minutes. Serves 5 to 6.

Knobby Kohlrabi

1 T. peanut or other oil   2 T. chopped fresh parsley
1 lb. kohlrabi, peeled & diced   ½ C. chicken stock or bouillon
½ tsp. sugar

Place oil in skillet over low heat. When hot, add all ingredients and cook, covered for 25 to 30 minutes until kohlrabi is tender.

Mary's French Fried Onion Rings

1 large onion   ⅔ C. milk
1 C. cornmeal   Oil for frying
2 eggs, beaten

Cut cleaned onion into ½-inch slices; separate rings. Soak in cold water for 20 minutes. Beat together cornmeal, eggs, and milk. Drain onions, dredge with cornmeal, dip into batter. Fry in hot oil and drain on brown paper or paper towels. Serve hot.

Mashed Parsnips

2 C. peeled & chopped   2 T. milk or cream
   parsnips   2 T. butter, divided
¼ tsp. salt   Dash of nutmeg

Simmer parsnips in boiling salted water for 15 to 20 minutes until tender. Drain and mash with potato masher or blender. Stir in cream and 1 T. butter. Pour into warm serving dish and top with 1 T. of butter and a brief sprinkle of nutmeg. Serves 2 to 3.

Mashed Potatoes with Apple

Mashed potatoes, leftover   Buttered crumbs
½ as much cooked apples as potatoes

Measure mashed potatoes. Mash cooked apples, drain well and measure ½ the amount of mashed potatoes. Stir to combine. Top with buttered crumbs. Place in heat-proof bowl and warm in 350° oven or heat in microwave.

Playin' post office is funner than cookin'.

Oven Onions

4 onions, peeled   Salt
4 bouillon cubes

Using a paring knife, make a depression in top of onion large enough to hold a chicken bouillon cube. Wrap in foil and bake for 50 to 60 minutes. Baste 3 or 4 times during baking. These onions can be roasted on the grill.

Nettie's Corn and Tomatoes

1 (No. 2) can whole tomatoes
  and juice
1 C. cooked whole kernel corn

¼ C. chopped onion
½ tsp. sugar
Optional: 1½ slices bread
  (more or less) to "thicken"

Boil tomatoes, corn, onion, and sugar for 5 to 6 minutes until onion is cooked. Tear bread into chunks and stir with vegetables if thickening is desired. Serves 4.

Pan Fried Eggplant

1 eggplant
1 egg
Flour

½ tsp. salt
Bacon fat or oil

Peel and slice eggplant. Soak for 30 minutes in salty water; drain. Dip slices in egg, then in flour. Fry in hot fat until brown. Turn and brown other side. Place on paper towels. Serves 5 to 6.

Cavortin' is funner than cookin'. . .

Peas and Celery

1 (10 oz.) pkg. frozen peas
¾ C. sliced celery

2 T. butter
¼ tsp. crushed dried thyme

Cook peas and drain well. Put butter in skillet over medium heat. Cook and stir celery 3 to 4 minutes. Celery should be crisp—tender. Stir peas and celery together. Serves 4.

Perfect Baked Potatoes

Potatoes
Cooking oil

Butter
Salt & pepper

Try to have potatoes nearly uniform in size. Scrub and dry potatoes. Make 2 or 3 small slits in each potato. Rub potatoes with oil. Bake at 375° for 60 minutes or until tender when pierced with sharp fork. When potatoes are done, cut X on top and press open. Top with butter, salt, and pepper or any favorite topping.

Pineapple Sweet Potato Bake

3 medium sweet potatoes
3 T. melted butter

1 small can crushed pineapple
½ tsp. salt

Boil unpeeled sweet potatoes until tender; peel and slice into buttered casserole. Spoon pineapple over sweet potatoes; sprinkle with melted butter and salt. Bake at 350° until light brown and pineapple juice has thickened.

Potato Pancakes

2 medium potatoes, shredded
1 carrot, grated
1 onion, minced

⅓ C. flour
2 eggs

Combine vegetables. Stir in flour, add beaten egg. Cook on lightly greased griddle or skillet for about 5 minutes on one side; turn and flatten pancake with spatula. Cook an additional 5 to 6 minutes.

Sauteed Green Tomatoes

½ C. flour
5 medium green tomatoes,
   sliced ½-inch thick

5 T. bacon drippings
   or cooking oil
Black pepper

Flour both sides of tomatoes and fry in hot drippings in oil until browned and tender. Pepper liberally. Really delicious with meats.

Turnip Greens and Pot Likker

¾ lb. salt pork
3 qts. water

Turnip greens
Salt and pepper

Simmer pork in the water for 50 to 60 minutes. Wash turnip greens several times to remove all grit. Add turnip greens to pot and cook for 1 hour. Drain and chop greens; season. Pour into hot dish and top with slices of pork. Serve with corn bread.

Turnips in All Their Glory

3 C. sliced turnips   1 T. parsley, chopped
3 T. butter   3 T. water
1 T. sugar

Melt butter in skillet. Add turnips, water, and sugar. Stir well. Cover and cook, stirring often for about 6 minutes or until turnips are tender. Remove lid and cook until almost dry. Serves 5 to 6.

Zucchini Romano

4 C. sliced zucchini   1 large tomato, chopped
1 C. onion rings   2 T. Romano cheese, grated
4 T. butter

Stir-fry zucchini and onions in butter 8 to 10 minutes. Add tomatoes and cook another 4 minutes. Pour into warm serving dish and sprinkle with Romano cheese.

Zucchini Plus

3 C. zucchini, sliced   2 T. butter or margarine
½ C. onion rings   Salt
2 C. carrot sticks

Stir-fry carrots in butter or margarine for 3 minutes; add zucchini, onions, and salt. Continue cooking until vegetables are crisp-tender. Salt, to taste.

Zucchini Annabel

1½ lbs. zucchini, thinly sliced   ¾ tsp. fennel
2 T. olive oil   ½ tsp. salt
1 onion, sliced

Wash and trim zucchini. Fry with onion in hot olive oil until lightly browned. Stir in fennel and salt. Cook an additional 3 to 4 minutes or longer. I like my zucchini crisp.

Playin' the piano is funner than cookin'. . .

Cold Green Beans Sesame

½ lb. green beans
Water
1 T. sugar

2 T. soy sauce
4 T. sesame seeds

Cut green beans on the diagonal. Cook for about 10 minutes in water until beans are not quite tender. Smash sesame seeds with side of cleaver. Place in bowl; add sugar and soy sauce, stirring until sugar is dissolved. Add green beans to bowl and toss well.

Sauerkraut Salad

4 C. sauerkraut
¾ C. chopped celery
½ C. chopped onion

1 C. sugar
½ C. salad oil

Combine sauerkraut, celery, and onion. Stir together salad oil, and sugar. Toss all together to coat kraut. Pack tightly in pint jars. Store in the refrigerator.

Swede Potatoes

1 medium rutabaga
3 T. butter
Water

¼ tsp. salt
Optional: 2 tsp. chopped parsley

Peel rutabaga and cut into pieces about ½-inch square. Put in saucepan with salt and water to cover. Cook, covered for about 20 minutes until tender. Add butter and sprinkle with parsley, if desired.

Spinach De Luxe

1 lb. spinach
1 tsp. salt
1 apple, chopped

1 carrot, grated
½ tsp. lemon juice

Wash spinach. In large kettle cook spinach in water clinging to leaves; add salt. Cook for 6 to 7 minutes until crisp-tender. Add apple, carrot, and lemon juice. Simmer until heated through. Serves 5 to 6.

Broccoli Celery Casserole

2 (10 oz. ea.) pkgs. frozen
   broccoli, cooked & drained
1 can condensed cream of
   celery soup

½ C. milk
¾ C. shredded sharp Cheddar
   cheese
¼ C. buttered crumbs

Place broccoli in 10x6x2-inch baking dish or pan. Stir together the soup, milk, and cheese. Pour this over broccoli and top with crumbs. Bake at 350° for 25 to 35 minutes. It should be bubbling.

Preserves and Sauces

Almond Sauce

5 T. butter   1 T. lemon juice
½ C. slivered almonds

Melt butter in heavy skillet; add the almonds and stir until lightly browned. Remove from heat, add lemon juice, and stir to combine. This is delicious on fish or vegetables.

Belle Pepper Sauce

4 bell peppers   3 T. bouillon or broth
4 medium onions, sliced   Salt
2 tsp. olive oil

Clean peppers and cut into strips. Saute' peppers and onions in oil for 6 to 8 minutes. Add bouillon or broth and cook and stir another 2 to 3 minutes. Salt, to taste. Nice served over plain rice or noodles. Serves 4.

This is Belle!

Canned Apricot Preserves

3 (1 lb. ea.) cans sweetened   2 T. lemon juice
   apricots   10 maraschino cherries
2 C. sugar

Drain fruit and reserve 1 C. apricot syrup. Mash apricots in blender or with masher; chop cherries. Add sugar and lemon juice in saucepan. Cook over low heat until thickened. Makes 1½ pints.

Chicken Gravy

3 T. fat from pan   1½ C. milk
3 T. flour   Salt & pepper

Pour fat from pan and place 3 T. back in SAME pan. Stir in flour and add milk. As the gravy bubbles and thickens, scrape off all bits of cooked-on chicken and juice. Simmer over VERY low heat for about 10 minutes. Season, to taste. Serves 4.

Chocolate Peanut Butter Sauce For Ice Cream

¾ C. milk   ½ C. peanut butter
⅓ C. sugar   ½ C. skinned chopped peanuts
2 sq. semi-sweet chocolate

Combine milk, sugar, and chopped chocolate in small saucepan. Cook and stir until mixture boils. Remove from heat and blend in peanut butter with whisk; add chopped peanuts. If you like a thinner sauce, stir a little water into cold sauce. Serve warm over ice cream.

(150)

Chocolate Satin Sauce

1 (6 oz.) pkg. semi-sweet
  chocolate chips
⅔ C. light corn syrup

6 oz. can evaporated milk
Optional: ½ C. chopped nuts

Combine chocolate chips and corn syrup in small heavy skillet or saucepan; cook and stir over very low heat until chocolate melts. Allow to cool. Stir in evaporated milk. Serve warm or cold on ice cream or other desserts.

Cranberry Orange Relish

1 orange
1 C. sugar

2 C. raw cranberries
½ C. nuts

Cut orange into quarters and remove seeds. Discard peel from 3 sections. Combine orange and sugar in blender; run on low speed until pureed. Pour into bowl. Add nuts and 1 C. cranberries. Run blender on high until cranberries are chopped; empty. Put second cup of cranberries in blender container. Run on high until coarsely chopped. Makes 1½ cups.

Cream of Mushroom Sauce

1 T. finely chopped onion
1 T. butter
1 (10¾ oz.) can cream of
   mushroom soup

4 T. milk
½ C. dry sherry

Fry onion in butter over low heat until golden, but not browned. Add mushroom soup and stir. Slowly stir in milk and sherry until mixture boils.

Creamy Horseradish Sauce for Fish

½ C. salad dressing or
   mayonnaise
½ C. catsup

½ tsp. sugar
1 T. horseradish
½ tsp. lemon juice

Put the horseradish in a sieve and press out excess moisture. Combine all ingredients. Store in the refrigerator.

Horseradish Sauce for Meat

¾ C. whipping cream
5 T. prepared horseradish,
   drained

¾ tsp. salt

Press horseradish to drain out as much liquid as possible. Fold the horseradish into the whipped cream and stir in salt. Try this with roast pork.

Dried Apricot Conserve

½ lb. dried apricots
1 small orange, unpeeled
1 (8 oz.) can crushed pineapple

3 C. sugar
¾ C. nuts, chopped

Wash apricots and soak overnight in water to cover. In this same water, cook apricots until tender and mash thoroughly. Remove seeds from orange and grind, rind and all. Combine all ingredients and bring to a boil, stirring frequently. Cook until thickened, taking care that mixture doesn't stick. Pour into sterilized half-pint containers and seal. Makes 4 half pints.

Hot Fudge Ice Cream
Pie Topping

1 (12 oz.) can evaporated milk
1 stick margarine
3 (1 oz. ea.) sq. unsweetened
  baking chocolate

2 C. sugar
1½ tsp. vanilla

Combine milk, butter, chocolate, and sugar in heavy saucepan. Cook over medium heat, stirring constantly with wooden spoon, about 5 to 10 minutes. Mixture will thicken.

Remove from heat and add vanilla. Cool sauce and smooth over ice cream pie. This can be served warm on ice cream and other desserts. Makes 3 cups.

(153)

Lemon Butter

½ C. butter, room temperature
1 tsp. grated lemon peel
3 T. chopped parsley
1½ tsp. dry tarragon
1 T. plus 1 tsp. lemon juice

Beat until well blended. Makes ½
cup. Pour over baked or broiled fish.

Milk Gravy

2 C. milk
3 T. flour
¼ tsp. salt

4 to 6 T. pan drippings from
chicken, steak, bacon,
chops, etc.

Heat drippings in skillet meat was cooked in; add flour. Stir and brown flour
very lightly. Add milk a little at a time, stirring constantly; add salt.

Onion Pasta Sauce

5 medium onions, sliced
½ C. cooking oil
2 T. tomato paste
¼ tsp. salt
1 tsp. sugar

Place oil and onions in a heavy skillet. Cover and cook over VERY low heat until almost like puree, being careful they don't burn. Stir or shake pan occasionally. After 25 minutes add the remaining ingredients and a little water. Simmer an additional 10 minutes. Serve over noodles. Enough for 4 to 5 servings.

Kickin' is funner than you know what . . .

Peach Apple Conserve

2 C. peeled & chopped peaches
2 C. unpeeled & chopped
  red apple

2 T. maraschino cherries, minced
½ C. fresh lemon juice
3 C. sugar

Combine all ingredients in heavy saucepan. Cook over low heat 20 to 30 minutes until apples are transparent. Pour into hot sterilized jars and seal at once.

Rhubarb Jam

2½ lbs. rhubarb, sliced thin
1 C. water   1 box Sure-Jell
6 C. sugar   ½ tsp. margarine

Combine rhubarb and water in pan. Simmer, covered for about 12 minutes or until rhubarb is soft.

Measure 4½ cups cooked rhubarb; pour into saucepan. Add 1 box Sure-Jell. Bring to a rolling boil (the boiling cannot be stirred down). Add sugar and bring to a boil, stirring constantly with wooden spoon. Continue boiling and stirring for 1 minute. Remove from heat and skim off foam. Pour immediately into sterilized jars. Wipe tops clean and cover with sterilized lids.

Scandia Sour Cream Sauce

1 C. sour cream   1 cucumber
3 T. chopped fresh dill   1 T. minced pimento

Stir chopped dill into sour cream. Add chopped and drained cucumber and pimento. Stir to combine and refrigerate. Serve on green salad or fish. Makes 1½ cups.

Tartar Sauce

1 C. mayonnaise
4 T. minced onion
¼ C. pickle relish
1 T. sweet pickle juice

Combine all ingredients and chill until serving time or overnight. Makes 1½ cups.

Chattin' is funner than cookin'.

Tomato Sauce for Noodles

¼ C. chopped green onion & tops
2 T. bacon fat

1½ tsp. savory
pepper, to taste

Fry onion in bacon fat until golden. Add tomatoes; crush savory with fingers and add with pepper. Cook for 4 minutes. Very good served on cooked noodles. Serves 2 or 3.

Whipped Cream Dressing

1 C. whipping cream
2 T. sugar

1 tsp. vanilla
2 T. mayonnaise

Have bowl and beaters cold. Whip cream until it forms soft peaks. Fold in sugar, vanilla, and mayonnaise. Whip a little longer. Use on fruit salads.

Cinnamon Cream Sauce

1 C. sugar
½ C. light corn syrup
¼ C. water

½ tsp. cinnamon
½ C. evaporated milk

Combine sugar, corn syrup, water, and cinnamon in small saucepan. Bring to a boil and cook and stir for 2 minutes. Remove from heat and cool for 5 minutes. Stir in evaporated milk. Serve warm on waffles or pancakes.

Chive Parsley Butter Sauce

1 T. chopped chives
1 T. chopped fresh parsley

½ tsp. salt
¼ C. melted butter or margarine

Melt butter over low heat or in microwave oven. Stir in remaining ingredients. Serve hot over cooked vegetables.

Miscellaneous

Substitute for Sweetened Condensed Milk

1 C. dry milk powder
⅔ C. sugar

⅓ C. boiling water
3 T. margarine

Combine all ingredients in blender. Substitute this for one can sweetened condensed milk. This is a real money saver.

Spanish Rice, Quick and Easy

6 slices bacon,
  cut in small pieces
5 T. chopped green pepper

1⅓ C. instant rice
1 env. dry onion soup mix
1 (No. 2½) can tomatoes

Fry the bacon, drain off ½ of the grease, then add green pepper and rice. Stir-fry until rice is coated. Add the dry onion soup mix and tomatoes. Bring to a boil, cover, and simmer for 5 to 6 minutes. Juice should be absorbed. Serves 4 to 6.

(159)

Monday's Sausage and Egg Surprise

¾ lb. highly seasoned sausage
5 eggs (4 hard-cooked, 1 raw)

1 tube refrigerator
  crescent rolls

Peel the 4 hard-cooked eggs. Divide the sausage into 4 pieces and shape a piece of the sausage around each egg so that it is completely covered.

Press 2 triangles of dough together to form a rectangle. Place an egg in the center of a square of dough. Pat water on edges of pastry to moisten. Pull corners of pastry to top of egg and seal. Egg should be completely covered with dough. Press edges to seal and trim off excess dough at top. Place sealed top down on lightly greased baking pan.

Roll out leftover dough on lightly floured board to about ¼-inch thick. Cut with small cutters to form decorations, or using sharp knife, cut leaf designs.

Beat egg; using pastry brush or fingers, glaze each wrapped egg. Press on designs and glaze. Make a small slit near bottom to let steam escape.

Bake at 375° for 10 minutes; lower heat to 350° and bake an additional 25 to 35 minutes. Watch closely as they brown very quickly.

These are great for any meal, hot or cold. I like them best cold. They're great for sack lunches and picnics, too.

Spiced Peaches

1 (30 oz.) can sweetened white
    cling peaches
1 T. vinegar

2-inches stick cinnamon,
    broken
1 tsp. whole cloves

Place all ingredients in a saucepan. Bring to a boil and simmer 5 to 6 minutes.
Pour in a small enough container that juice covers the peaches. Store in the
refrigerator overnight before using.

Spanish Rice

2 T. olive oil
1 C. long-grain rice
½ tsp. sugar

1 to 2 tsp. chili powder
2 C. water

Place olive oil and rice in skillet. Saute' until golden brown. Stir sugar and
chili powder into water to dissolve. Pour over rice and stir. Cover and cook
over low heat until moisture is absorbed, about 20 minutes. Serves 2 to 3.

Spiced Stewed Prunes

1 lb. prunes
2 cloves
3 T. sugar

½ lemon, thinly
    sliced & seeded

Cover prunes with water and let soak overnight. Drain and add water to almost
cover. Add sugar, cloves, and lemon. Cook for 10 to 15 minutes. Try these
on people who say they don't like prunes.

Simple Syrup

1 C. sugar   ½ C. water

Cook, stirring constantly until sugar is dissolved. Bring to a rolling boil. Cool and refrigerate. Use this to sweeten cold drinks.

Nuts dipped in simple syrup WILL STICK TO COOKIES.

Slumgullion

I'm not sure how you spell the name of this recipe, but my brother-in-law's mother made it many, many years ago when she lived in Dallas City, Illinois.

1 (7 oz.) pkg. macaroni   1 tsp. Worcestershire sauce
2 T. butter or oil   1½ C. shredded sharp,
½ C. chili sauce   processed cheese

Cook macaroni according to package directions. Drain, then return to saucepan. Add butter or margarine, chili sauce, and Worcestershire sauce. Stir together and add cheese.

Snow Pea Soup

3 C. chicken stock with pieces   ¼ C. chopped carrot
  of chicken   1½ C. snow peas, cut into
4 T. chopped green onions   bite-size pieces

Combine all ingredients. Bring to a boil and simmer over low heat until snow peas are tender, 15 to 20 minutes. Salt, to taste. Serves 4.

Red Radish Relish

35 small red radishes	¾ tsp. vinegar
1½ tsp. seasoned salt	2 T. chives
½ C. sour cream	

Chop radishes or put in blender with a little water. Buzz on medium until radishes are well chopped. Place paper towels in colander and pour in radishes; allow to drain for 1 hour. Press to extract as much water as possible.

In bowl combine cream, vinegar, and chives. Stir to blend. Add radishes and refrigerate. Serve with meat or pile on snack crackers.

Rice De Luxe

1 C. rice	1 jar mushrooms with stems,
1 stick butter or margarine	chopped
1 onion, chopped	2 C. water

Stir rice in butter over low heat until rice browns; add onion. Combine all ingredients in greased baking dish with lid. Bake at 350° for 1 hour. Serves 5 to 6.

(163)

Pickled Nasturtium Seeds, "Capers"

1 C. fresh green
   nasturtium seeds
½ C. water

⅓ tsp. salt
½ C. sugar
½ C. cider vinegar

Rinse seeds several times; drain and put in crock or glass bowl. Stir water and salt together; pour over the seeds. Cover and let sit for 2 days. Drain seeds and pour into sterilized glass jar. Bring sugar and vinegar to boiling; pour over seeds and seal. Makes 1 cup.

Used chopped "capers" in sauce for fish or in salad dressing.

Quick Chicken Soup

2 C. chicken broth or
   2 bouillon cubes
½ to ¾ C. cooked or fresh
   chopped chicken

½ C. chopped raw or
   cooked vegetables
1 T. onion, chopped

If using bouillon, pour 2 C. boiling water over cubes. Add chicken and vegetables to broth or bouillon. If ingredients are cooked, simmer 4 to 5 minutes. If uncooked, simmer until vegetables are tender. Serves 2 to 3.

Knox Gelatin Cut Ups

4 env. Knox unflavored gelatin   4 C. water
3 (3 oz. ea.) pkgs. any flavor gelatin

Combine the gelatins, add boiling water and stir to completely dissolve. Pour into a 9x13-inch shallow pan. Refrigerate until firm. Kids have fun making animal cut-outs with this.

Low Calorie "Maple" Syrup

⅓ C. sugar   1 C. cold water
1 T. cornstarch   2 tsp. maple extract
1/8 tsp. salt

Combine sugar, cornstarch, salt, and water in small pan. Cook and stir over medium heat until bubbly and thickened. Lower heat and cook for 1 minute. Remove from heat; add maple extract and stir. Store in the refrigerator. Makes 1 cup.

Pome and Raisin Relish

1 C. applesauce   ½ tsp. dried majoram, crushed
½ C. raisins, soaked   1 T. maraschino cherries, chopped
2 T. grated orange peel

Combine all ingredients and stir; refrigerate. Serve this relish with pork or Danish open-face sandwiches. Makes 1½ cups.

Homestyle Noodles for Chop Suey

½ lb. very fine noodles   ¾ tsp. salt
1 T. plus 2 tsp. cooking oil

Cook noodles according to package directions. Drain and chill thoroughly.
Place oil in a heavy skillet. When hot, add noodles and fry until lightly browned.

Many of my Oriental friends prefer these rather than the all-crisp noodles,
because they're like Mama used to make.

Hot Mustard for Chop Suey
and Other Chinese Dishes

4 T. dry mustard   Dry white wine
2 tsp. soy sauce

Place mustard in small bowl; add soy sauce. Gradually add wine, stirring
with a fork to make a thin paste. Let sit 15 minutes to develop flavor. Use
sparingly.

A little of this on top of some chop suey when you have a cold will clear
your head in a hurry.

Elephant Stew

1 elephant
2 rabbits

3 sacks salt
½ sack pepper

Have butcher cut elephant into small pieces. Make a lot of gravy so you have enough to cover the pieces. Cook on kerosene stove for 4 months.

This stew serves 4000 to 4006 people. If unexpected guests turn up, add the 2 rabbits, but only if necessary as most people do not like to find hare in their stew.

Fried Apples

4 red-skinned apples
¼ C. raisins

2 T. oil or bacon fat

Core and slice apples. Fry apples in oil or bacon fat 10 to 15 minutes; add raisins and stir. Serve with pork chops or ham.

If you're calorie counting, "fry" apples with 2 to 3 T. water. Unbelievably good!

Dijonnie Mustard

4 ozs. dry mustard
3 cloves
½ tsp. salt

1 T. onion juice
1 C. very dry white wine

Stir together mustard, cloves, and salt. Add onion juice. Add wine gradually to make a paste and stir until smooth. Store in refrigerator. Makes a little over 1 cup. Refrigerate in covered jar.

Wind skatin' is funner than cookin'.

Egg Glaze

1 egg

2 tsp. water

Beat egg and water together. Using a pastry brush, coat unbaked breads, cookies and top of your pie crusts for a rich golden color.

(168)

Chocolate Cake Cones

1 pkg. Jiffy one-layer dark
  fudge cake
1 egg

½ C. water
14 flat-bottomed cones

Prepare cake as directed on package. Pour scant ¼ C. batter into 14 flat-bottomed cones. Cones should be a scant ½ full. Place cones upright in muffin tin or in cookie sheet. Bake at 350° for 15 to 20 minutes. Can be frosted with your favorite icing.

Cream Fruit Pops

3 C. fruit juice, any kind
Sugar, if juice is tart

12 T. cream
Sticks (tongue depressors)

Combine ingredients. If sugar is used, stir to dissolve. Pour into 2 plastic popsicle molds, or pour into narrow jelly glasses. When ''pops'' are slushy, insert sticks. This can also be frozen in ice cube trays with toothpicks for ''holders''.

Deviled Eggs

6 hard-cooked eggs, peeled
3 T. pickle relish, pressed dry
3 tsp. mayonnaise or mustard or
  combination of both

Salt, to taste
Parsley sprigs

Cut eggs lengthwise. Mash yolks, add relish, mayonnaise or mustard and salt; stir to combine. Fill the whites and garnish with small sprigs of parsley.

Basic Cooked Rice

Cooking rice is so simple, I rarely ever buy instant. Try it.

1 C. rice, not instant   Optional: ¾ tsp. salt
2 C. water

In pot with a lid, bring rice and water to a full boil; add salt if using, turn down heat, cover the kettle, and simmer for 20 minutes.

If all the water is not absorbed, continue cooking for a few more minutes. Let sit for 10 minutes. Stir to fluff before serving. Makes 3 cups of cooked rice.

Beef Jerky, Microwave

1½ lbs. beef (flank or top round)   ¾ tsp. garlic salt
1½ tsp. salt   ½ tsp. black pepper

Cut steak lengthwise (with grain) into 1/8-inch thick strips. Combine salt, garlic salt, and pepper.

Arrange half the strips flat and close together on microwave-safe bacon rack. Cover with waxed paper and microwave at Medium Low 21 minutes; invert strips, placing drier strips in center of the rack; rotate back ½ turn and continue microwaving at Medium Low another 21 minutes until meat is dry, but slightly pliable. Remove to absorbent paper. Repeat with remaining strips.

Store in covered container in the refrigerator.

Lupe's Chili Dumplings

1 ½ C. self-rising flour   ¾ C. tomato juice
¾ tsp. chili powder

Stir chili powder into flour; stir in tomato juice.

Drop by tablespoons over simmering cooked beef stew. Cover and simmer for 15 minutes. Do not lift the lid. This makes 8 to 10 dumplings.

Spaghetti with Peanuts

¼ lb. spaghetti, cooked
3 T. butter
2 C. ground roasted peanuts
2 T. flour
2 C. milk

Butter a casserole with 1 T. of the butter.

Make a sauce using 2 T. butter, flour, and milk. Stir in the peanuts and pour over the spaghetti; toss to mix.

Bake at 350° for 40 to 50 minutes.

Tippy toe'n in the moonlight is funner than cookin'.

Antonia's Chili and Tamales

2 (1 lb. ea.) cans chili with beans
1 (1 lb.) can tamales,
  unwrapped

¼ C. onion, chopped
½ C. Cheddar cheese,
  shredded

Pour chili and beans into a 1½-quart casserole dish and arrange tamales on top. Sprinkle with onions and cheese. Bake at 350° for 25 to 30 minutes.

Iowa Fried Peaches

8 large peaches
3 T. butter

1 T. dark brown sugar
Vanilla ice cream

Peel, halve the peaches, and remove seeds. Cut thin slice off rounded side of peach to level. Melt the butter in a large skillet and put in the peaches, leveled side down. Fill hollows with brown sugar. Simmer, covered until just beginning to get soft. Serve with a scoop of vanilla ice on top of each peach half.

Yam Crispy Chips

6 yams
Water

Peanut oil, or other
  for frying

Peel yams and slice on thinly as possible. Soak chips for 4 hours. Drain and pat dry with cloth or paper towels. Heat oil to 400° and cook chips to a golden brown; drain. Sprinkle with salt and enjoy!

Yorkshire Pudding

½ C. hot beef roast drippings
2 eggs
1 C. milk

1 C. flour
½ tsp. salt

Pour hot beef drippings into a 9x9x2-inch pan. Beat together eggs and milk; add the flour and salt; beat again. Pour over hot drippings in pan and bake at 425° for 30 to 40 minutes. Pudding should be a deep, golden brown. Serve at once with roast beef. Serves 6 to 9.

Cattin' around is funner than cookin'.

Sausage Meat Balls with Rice

1½ lbs. bulk sausage
1 large onion, sliced
3 C. cooked rice

1 C. diced celery
1¾ tsp. salt

Shape sausage into small balls and cook in Dutch oven until nicely brown-ed, about 12 minutes. Remove and reserve. Pour off all but about 2 T. of fat. Add onion and rice; cook and stir until golden. Add sausage balls, celery, and salt.

I think I'd rather cook . . .

Need A Gift?

For

- Shower • Birthday • Mother's Day •
  • Anniversary • Christmas •

Turn Page for Order Form
(Order Now While Supply Lasts!)

To Order Copies Of

Funner Things To Do Cookbook

Please send me _____ copies of **Funner Things To Do Cookbook** at $11.95 each. (Make checks payable to **QUIXOTE PRESS**.)

Name _____

Street _____

City _____State _____Zip _____

Quixote Press
1854 - 345th Ave.
Wever, IA 52658
800-571-2665

- -

To Order Copies Of

Funner Things To Do Cookbook

Please send me _____ copies of **Funner Things To Do Cookbook** at $11.95 each. (Make checks payable to **QUIXOTE PRESS**.)

Name _____

Street _____

City _____State _____Zip _____

Quixote Press
1854 - 345th Ave.
Wever, IA 52658
800-571-2665

(176)

STANDARD ABBREVIATIONS

tsp. - teaspoon
T. - tablespoon
C. - cup
f.g. - few grains
pt. - pint
qt. - quart

d.b. - double boiler
B.P. - baking powder
oz. - ounce
lb. - pounds
pk. - peck
bu. - bushel

GUIDE TO WEIGHTS AND MEASURES

1 teaspoon - 60 drops
3 teaspoons - 1 tablespoon
2 tablespoons - 1 fluid ounce
4 tablespoons - ¼ cup
5⅓ tablespoons - ⅓ cup
8 tablespoons - ½ cup
16 tablespoons - 1 cup

1 pound - 16 ounces
1 cup - ½ pint
2 cups - 1 pint
4 cups - 1 quart
4 quarts - 1 gallon
8 quarts - 1 peck
4 pecks - 1 bushel

SUBSTITUTIONS AND EQUIVALENTS

2 tablespoons of fat - 1 ounce
1 cup of fat - ½ pound
1 pound of butter -2 cups
1 cup of hydrogenated fat plus ½ t. salt - 1 cup butter
2 cups sugar - 1 pound
2½ cups packed brown sugar - 1 pound
1⅓ cups packed brown sugar - 1 cup of granulated sugar
3½ cups of powdered sugar - 1 pound
4 cups sifted all-purpose flour - 1 pound
4½ cups sifted cake flour - 1 pound
1 ounce bitter chocolate - 1 square
4 tablespoons cocoa plus 2 teaspoon butter - 1 ounce of bitter chocolate
1 cup egg whites - 8 to 10 whites
1 cup egg yolks - 12 to 14 yolks
16 marshmallows - ¼ pound
1 tablespoon cornstarch - 2 tablespoons flour for thickening
1 tablespoon vinegar or lemon juice + 1 cup milk - 1 cup sour milk
10 graham crackers - 1 cup fine crumbs
1 cup whipping cream - 2 cups whipped
1 cup evaporated milk - 3 cups whipped
1 lemon - 3 to 4 tablespoons juice
1 orange - 6 to 8 tablespoons juice
1 cup uncooked rice - 3 to 4 cups cooked rice

SUBSTITUTIONS

FOR	YOU CAN USE. . .
1 T. cornstarch	2 T. flour OR 1½ T. quick cooking tapioca
1 C. cake flour	1 C. less 2 T. all-purpose flour
1 C. all-purpose flour	1 C. plus 2 T. cake flour
1 sq. chocolate	3 T. cocoa & 1 T. fat
1 C. melted shortening	1 C. salad oil (may not be substituted for solid shortening)
1 C. milk	½ C. evaporated milk & ½ C. water
1 C. sour milk or buttermilk	1 T. lemon juice or vinegar & enough sweet milk to measure 1 C.
1 C. heavy cream	⅔ C. milk & ⅓ C. butter
Sweetened condensed milk	No substitution
1 egg	2 T. dried whole egg & 2 T. water
1 tsp. baking powder	¼ tsp. baking soda & 1 tsp. cream of tartar OR ¼ tsp. baking soda & ½ C. sour milk, buttermilk or molasses; reduce other liquid ½ C.
1 C. sugar	1 C. honey; reduce other liquid ¼ C.; reduce baking temperature by 25°
1 C. miniature marshmallows	About 10 large marshmallows (cut-up)
1 medium onion (2½-inch diameter)	2 T. instant minced onion OR 1 tsp. onion powder OR 2 T. onion salt; reduce salt 1 tsp.
1 garlic clove	1/8 tsp. garlic powder OR ¼ tsp. garlic salt; reduce salt 1/8 tsp.
1 T. fresh herbs	1 tsp. dried herbs OR ¼ tsp. powdered herbs OR ½ tsp. herb salt; reduce salt ¼ tsp.

Protein Content and Caloric Value of Foods for Your Diet

Food	Oz.	Approximate Measure	Protein	Calories
Lamb				
Chops				
Loin or				
rib	4	1 loin or 2 rib 1-inch thick	17.9	421
Shoulder	4	Piece 4x3x5/8-inch	18.7	348
Roasts				
Leg	4	Slice 4x3x½-inch	21.6	276
Shoulder	4	Slice 5x3x½-inch	18.7	348
Pork, fresh				
Chops and steaks				
Leg (ham)	4	Piece 3½x3x½-inch	18.2	408
Loin	4	Chop ¾-inch thick	19.7	349
Shoulder	4	Piece 4½x3½x3/8-inch	16.1	464
Roasts				
Boston butt	4	Slice 4½x3½x3/8-inch	19.9	327
Loin	4	Slice ¾-inch thick	19.7	349
Tenderloin	4	2 pieces 1-inch dia.x3-inches long	23.9	172
Pork, cured				
Bacon,				
Canadian				
style	1	Slice 2¼-inch diameter by 3/16-inch thick	6.6	68
Ham				
(boiled)	2	Slice 4¼x4x1/8-inch	10.6	147
Veal				
Chops				
Loin	4	Chop 5/8-inch thick	23.0	211
Rib	4	Chop ¾-inch thick	22.6	241
Roasts				
Leg	4	Slice 4x2½x½-inch	22.9	223
Loin	4	Slice 4x2½x½-inch	23.0	211
Rib	4	Slice 4x2½x½-inch	22.6	241
Shoulder	4	Slice 5x3x½-inch	23.3	202
Steaks				
Cutlet				
(round)	4	Piece 4x2½x½-inch	23.4	191
Shoulder	4	Piece 5x3x½-inch	23.3	202
Sirloin	4	Piece 4x2½x½-inch	23.0	211
Stew				
(breast)	4	4 pieces 2½x1x1-inch	22.0	271
Variety Meats				
Brains (beef)	4	2 pieces 2½x1½x1-inch	12.6	152
Heart (avg.)	4	⅓ ht. 3-inch dia. x 3½-inch long	19.7	157
Kidney (avg.)	4	3 slices 3¼x2½x¼-inch	20.0	161
Liver				
Beef	3	2 slices 3x2½x3/8-inch	17.7	119
Lamb	3	2 slices 3½x2x3/8-inch	18.9	118
Pork	3	2 slices 3½x2x3/8-inch	17.7	116
Veal	3	2 slices 3x2½x3/8-inch	17.1	122
Sweetbread	4	Piece 4x3x¾-inch	18.2	216
Tongue	3	3 slices 3x2x¼-inch	15.7	191

Protein Content and Caloric Value of Foods for Your Diet

Food	Oz.	Approximate Measure	Protein	Calories
Sausages and Cooked Specialties				
Bologna	1	Slice 4½ dia. x ½-inch thick	4.4	65
Frankfurter	2	2 5½-inch long x ¾-inch dia.	9.1	121
Liver sausage	1	Slice 3-inch dia. x ¼-inch thick	5.0	77
Luncheon meat	1	Slice 4x3½x1/8-inch	4.6	81
Vienna sausage	1	2 pieces 2-inch long x ¾-inch diameter	5.8	76
Poultry				
Chicken				
Liver	3	4 avg.	19.9	122
Roast				
Breast	3	½ breast	21.0	110
Leg	2½	1 avg.	14.7	88
Thigh	2½	1 avg.	15.8	95
Wing	1	1 avg.	7.0	37
Stewed				
Dark meat	3½	½ cup (diced)	23.1	139
Light meat	3	½ cup (diced)	20.3	106
Turkey				
Roast				
Dark meat	3½	Slice 4x3x½-inch	23.2	177
Light meat	3½	Slice 4x3x½-inch	24.5	139
Fish				
Bass	4	1 small fish	27.3	113
Clams	3½	5 medium	12.8	77
Cod	3½	Piece 4x2¼x¾-inch	16.5	70
Crab (canned)	3	⅔ cup	16.1	94
Finnan haddie	3½	¾ cup	23.2	96
Flounder	3½	Piece 4x3x3/8-inch	19.0	79
Haddock	3½	Piece 3½x3x¾-inch	17.2	72
Halibut	4	Piece 4x3x½-inch	20.4	133
Herring, fresh	4	1 fish 7-inches long	22.8	163
Lobster				
Canned	3	½ cup	15.6	74
Fresh	2½	1 avg.	12.2	63
Mackerel	2½	¼ fish 7-inches long	14.3	119
Oysters	3½	5 medium	6.0	50
Perch	4	2 fish 4½-inches long	23.4	102
Salmon				
Canned	3½	⅔ cup	24.7	203
Fresh	3	Piece 2½x2½x7/8-inch	15.7	196
Shrimp (canned)	2	3/8 cup or 12 pieces 1-inch dia.	10.7	49
Trout	3	Piece 6-inches long	16.1	80
White fish	4	Piece 3¼-inchx3x½-inch	25.2	165
Milk and Dairy Products				
Butter	⅓		.1	73
Cheese, cottage	2	¼ cup	9.6	51
Cream, coffee	½	1 T.	.4	29

(180)

Protein Content and Caloric Value of Foods for Your Diet

Food	Approx. Weight (Oz.)	Approximate Measure (Gm.)	Protein	Calories
Milk				
Buttermilk	7	1 glass	7.0	72
Evaporated	4	½ cup	8.4	167
Skim	7	1 glass	7.0	72
Whole	7	1 glass	7.0	138
Eggs	1⅔	1 medium	6.4	79
Potatoes				
White	2	1 small 2½-inch long x 2-inch dia.	1.2	51
Vegetables				
Artichokes	3½	½ large	2.9	63
Asparagus	3½	7 stalks 6-inches long	2.3	27
Beans, string	3½	⅔ cup	2.4	42
Beet greens	3½	½ cup	2.0	33
Beets	3½	⅔ cup or 2 1¾-inch dia.	1.6	46
Broccoli	3½	2 stalks 5-inches long	3.3	37
Brussels sprts.	3½	⅔ cup	4.4	58
Cabbage	3½	1/5 head 4½-inch dia.	1.4	29
Carrots	3½	2 carrots 5-inch long	1.2	45
Cauliflower	3½	⅔ cup	2.4	31
Celery	½	Piece 8½-inch long or 2 hts.	.2	3
Chard, Swiss	3½	½ cup	1.4	25
Chicory	1	10 small leaves	.4	7
Cucumbers	2	8 slices 1/8-inch thick	.4	7
Eggplant	2	Slices 3½-inch dia x 3/8-inch thick	.7	17
Endive, French	2	2 stalks	.8	11
Green pepper	½	½ cup or piece 4x1¾-inch	.2	4
Kohlrabi	3½	⅔ cup (diced)	2.1	36
Lettuce				
Head	3½	¼ head 4-inch diameter	1.2	18
	½	1 leaf	.2	3
Leaf	½	2 leaves	.1	2
Mushrooms	3½	5 caps 2¼-inch dia.	2.6	15
Okra	2	5 pods	1.0	21
Onions				
Dried	3	1 onion 2-inch dia.	1.2	42
Green	½	3 medium	.2	7
Parsley		2 sprigs	.1	1
Pumpkin	3½	½ cup	1.2	36
Radishes	1	3 radishes 1-inch dia.	.4	7
Rutabagas	3½	½ cup	1.1	41
Sauerkraut	3½	⅔ cup	1.1	18
Spinach	3½	¾ cup	2.3	25
Squash				
Summer	3½	½ cup	.6	19
Winter	3½	½ cup	1. 5	44
Tomatoes				
Canned	3½	½ cup	1.2	25
Fresh	3½	1 tomato 2-inch dia.	1.0	23
Juice, canned	4	½ cup	1.2	28
Turnip greens	3½	½ cup	2.9	37

Protein Content and Caloric Value of Foods for Your Diet

Food	Oz.	Approximate Measure	Protein	Calories
Turnips				
White	3½	⅔ cup	1.1	35
Yellow (see	rutabagas)			
Pickles				
Olives				
Green	1/6	1 medium	.1	7
Ripe	½	1 large	.2	23
Pickles				
Dill	2	½ pickle 5-inches long x1½-inch diameter	.3	7
Sweet	½	1 pickle 2½-inches long x¾-inch diameter	.2	21
BREAD AND CEREAL PRODUCTS				
Cereals				
Bran, whole	⅔	⅓ cup	2.5	67
Cornflakes	½	⅔ cup	1.3	56
Farina, enriched	⅔	½ cup (sc. 2 T. dry)	2.3	71
Oatmeal	⅔	½ cup (¼ cup dry)	3.1	77
Rice				
Puffed	⅓	¾ cup	.7	36
White	1	⅔ cup (2 T. dry)	2.3	105
Wheat				
Flakes	⅔	¾ cup	2.4	74
Puffed	⅓	¾ cup	1.2	37
Shredded	1	1 biscuit	2.9	103
Breads				
Rye	⅔	Slice 4x3½x½-inch	1.2	50
Wheat				
Melba toast	1/6	Slice 3x2x¼-inch	.6	19
White, enrch	⅔	1 slice (commercial) thin	1.6	50
Whole wheat	⅔	1 slice (commercial) thin	1.8	50
Crackers				
Graham	½	1 cracker 3-inch square	1.0	54
Saltine	½	1 cracker 2-inch square	.4	17
Soda	1/5	1 cracker 2¾x2½-inch	.6	25
Zwieback	¼	1 piece 3¼x1¼x½-inch	.9	33
Beverages				
Carbonated	6	1 small bottle		82
Coffee, black			0	0
Tea, plain			0	0
Fruits				
Apples	3½	1 apple 2¼-inch diameter	.3	65
Apricots	1	1 medium	.4	20
Blackberries	3½	¾ cup	1.2	62
Blueberries	3½	⅔ cup	.6	68
Cantaloupe	4	¼ melon 5-inch diameter	.8	29
Cherries, sweet	3½	15 cherries 7/8-inch diameter	1.2	87
Grapefruit	3½	½ medium 3 5/8-inch dia.	.5	44
Grapes				
Concord	3½	34 avg.	1.4	78
Green seedless	3½	40 small	.8	74
Malaga or Tokay	3½	21 avg.	.8	74

Protein Content and Caloric Value of Foods for Your Diet

Honeydew melon	4	1½-inch slice, 7-inch melon	.9	48
Oranges	3½	½ orange 4-inch diameter	.9	52
Peaches	3½	1 medium	.5	51
Pears	3½	1 small	.7	70
Pineapple	3½	1 slice 4-inch diameter x ½-inch thick	.4	58
Plums	2½	1 plum 1¾-inch dia.	.5	39
Raspberries	3	⅔ cup	1.1	64
Strawberries	3½	10 strawberries 1-inch dia.	.8	41
Watermelon	5	½ slice 6-inch dia. x ¾-inch thick	.8	51
FRUIT JUICES				
Grapefruit, canned	4	½ cup	.6	49
Orange	4	½ cup	.7	66
Pineapple canned	4	½ cup	.4	65
Tomato (see	vegetables)			

HOW MANY DROPS IN A "DASH"?

Here, a cook's guide to the most-often-called-for
food measures and equivalents

How many cups of berries in a pint? How many slices of bread make a half cup of crumbs? For two tablespoons of orange peel, will you need more than one orange? You'll find the answers to these questions and lots more in this handy kitchen chart.

EQUIVALENT MEASURES

Dash	2 to 3 drops or less than 1/8 teaspoon
1 tablespoon	3 teaspoons
¼ cup	4 tablespoons
⅓ cup	5 tablespoons plus 1 teaspoon
½ cup	8 tablespoons
1 cup	16 tablespoons
1 pint	2 cups
1 quart	4 cups
1 gallon	4 quarts
1 peck	8 quarts
1 bushel	4 pecks
1 pound	16 ounces

FOOD EQUIVALENTS

Apples *1 pound*	3 medium (3 cups sliced)
Bananas *1 pound*	3 medium (1⅓ cups mashed)
Berries *1 pint*	1¾ cups
Bread *1 pound loaf*	14 to 20 slices
Bread crumbs, fresh *1 slice* *bread with crust*	½ cup bread crumbs
Broth, chicken or beef *1 cup*	1 bouillon cube or 1 envelope bouillon or 1 teaspoon instant bouillon dissolved in 1 cup boiling water
Butter or margarine *¼ pound stick*	½ cup
Cheese *¼ pound*	1 cup, shredded
Cheese, cottage *8 ounces*	1 cup
Cheese, cream *3 ounces*	6 tablespoons
Chocolate, unsweetened *1 ounce*	1 square
Chocolate, semi-sweet pieces *6 ounce package*	1 cup

(184)

QUANTITIES TO SERVE 100 PEOPLE

Coffee	—3 lbs.
Loaf Sugar	—3 lbs.
Cream	—3 qts.
Whipping Cream	—4 pts.
Milk	—6 gallons
Fruit	—2½ gallons
Fruit Juice	—4 (No. 10 ea.) cans (26 lbs.)
Tomato Juice	—4 (No. 10 ea.) cans (26 lbs.)
Soup	—5 gallons
Oysters	—18 qts.
Weiners	—25 lbs.
Meatloaf	—24 lbs.
Ham	—40 lbs.
Beef	—40 lbs.
Roast Pork	—40 lbs.
Hamburger	—30-36 lbs.
Chicken For Chicken Pie	—40 lbs.
Potatoes	—35 lbs.
Scalloped Potatoes	—5 gallon
Vegetables	—4 (No. 10 ea.) cans (26 lbs.)
Baked Beans	—5 gallon
Beets	—30 lbs.
Cauliflower	—18 lbs.
Cabbage For Slaw	—20 lbs.
Carrots	—33 lbs.
Bread	—10 loaves
Rolls	—200
Butter	—3 lbs.
Potato Salad	—12 qts.
Fruit Salad	—20 qts.
Vegetable Salad	—20 qts.
Lettuce	—20 heads
Salad Dressing	—3 qts.
Pies	—18
Cakes	—8
Ice Cream	—4 gallons
Cheese	—3 lbs.
Olives	—1¾ lbs.
Pickles	—2 qts.
Nuts	—3 lbs. sorted

To Serve 50 People, Divide by 2
To Serve 25 People, Divide by 4

(185)

THE KITCHEN
General Household Hints

SALT

If stew is too salty, add raw cut potatoes and discard once they have cooked and absorbed the salt. Another remedy is to add a teaspoon each of cider vinegar and sugar. Or, simply add sugar.

If soup or stew is too sweet, add salt. For a main dish or vegetable, add a teaspoon of cider vinegar.

GRAVY

For pale gravy, color with a few drops of Kitchen Bouquet. Or to avoid the problem in the first place, brown the flour well before adding the liquid. This also helps prevent lumpy gravy.

To make gravy smooth, keep a jar with a mixture of equal parts of flour and cornstarch. Put 3-4 T. of this mixture in another jar and add some water. Shake, and in a few minutes you will have a smooth paste for gravy.

To remedy greasy gravy, add a small amount of baking soda.

For quick thickener for gravies, add some instant potatoes to your gravy and it will thicken beautifully.

VEGETABLES

If fresh vegetables are wilted or blemished, pick off the brown edges. Sprinkle with cool water, wrap in towel and refrigerate for an hour or so.

Perk up soggy lettuce by adding lemon juice to a bowl of cold water and soak for an hour in the refrigerator.

Lettuce and celery will crisp up fast if you place it in a pan of cold water and add a few sliced potatoes.

If vegetables are overdone, put the pot in a pan of cold water. Let it stand from 15 minutes to ½ hour without scraping pan.

By lining the crisper section of your refrigerator with newspaper and wrapping vegetables with it, moisture will be absorbed and your vegetables will stay fresher longer.

(186)

EGGS

If you shake the egg and you hear a rattle, you can be sure it's stale.

If you are making deviled eggs and want to slice it perfectly, dip the knife in water first. The slice will be smooth with no yolk sticking to the knife.

The white of an egg is easiest to beat when it's at room temperature. So leave it out of the refrigerator about ½ hour before using it.

To make light and fluffy scrambled eggs, add a little water while beating the eggs.

Add vinegar to the water while boiling eggs. Vinegar helps to seal the egg, since it acts on the calcium in the shell.

To make quick-diced eggs, take your potato masher and go to work on a boiled egg.

If you wrap each egg in aluminum foil before boiling it, the shell won't crack when it's boiling.

To make those eggs go further when making scrambled eggs for a crowd, add a pinch of baking powder and 2 tsp. of water per egg.

A great trick for peeling eggs the easy way - when they are finished boiling, turn off the heat and just let them sit in the pan with the lid on for about 5 minutes. Steam will build up under the shell and they will just fall away.

Or, quickly rinse hot hard-boiled eggs in cold water, and the shells will be easier to remove.

When you have saved a lot of egg yolks from previous recipes; use them in place of whole eggs for baking or thickening. Just add 2 yolks for every whole egg.

Fresh or hard-boiled? Spin the egg. If it wobbles, it is raw - if it spins easily, it's hard-boiled.

Add a few drops of vinegar to the water when poaching an egg to keep it from running all over the pan.

Add 1 T. of water per egg white to increase the quantity of beaten egg white when making meringue.

Try adding eggshells to coffee after it has perked, for a better flavor.

POTATOES

Overcooked potatoes can become soggy when the milk is added. Sprinkle with dry powdered milk for the fluffiest mashed potatoes ever.

To hurry up baked potatoes, boil in salted water for 10 minutes, then place in a very hot oven. Or, cut potatoes in half and place them face down on a baking sheet in the oven to make the baking time shorter.

When making potato pancakes, add a little sour cream to keep potatoes from discoloring.

Save some of the water in which the potatoes were boiled - add to some powdered milk and use when mashing. This restores some of the nutrients that were lost in the cooking process.

Use a couple of tablespoons of cream cheese in place of butter for your potatoes; try using sour cream instead of milk when mashing.

ONIONS

To avoid tears when peeling onions, peel them under cold water or refrigerate before chopping.

For sandwiches to go in lunchboxes, sprinkle with dried onion. They will have turned into crisp pieces by lunchtime.

Peel and quarter onions. Place one layer deep in a pan and freeze. Quickly pack in bags or containers while frozen. Use as needed, chopping onions while frozen, with a sharp knife.

TOMATOES

Keep tomatoes in storage with stems pointed downward and they will retain their freshness longer.

Sunlight doesn't ripen tomatoes. It's the warmth that makes them ripen. So find a warm spot near the stove or dishwasher where they can get a little heat.

Save the juice from canned tomatoes in ice cube trays. When frozen, store in plastic bags in freezer for cooking use or for tomato drinks.

To improve the flavor of inexpensive tomato juice, pour a 46-ounce can of it into a refrigerator jar and add one chopped green onion and a cut-up stalk of celery.

ROCK-HARD BROWN SUGAR
Add a slice of soft bread to the package of brown sugar, close the bag tightly, and in a few hours the sugar will be soft again. If you need it in a hurry, simply grate the amount called for with a hand grater. Or, put brown sugar and a cup of water (do not add to the sugar, set it alongside of it) in a covered pan. Place in the oven (low heat) for awhile. Or, buy liquid brown sugar.

THAWING FROZEN MEAT
Seal the meat in a plastic bag and place in a bowl of very warm water. Or, put in a bag and let cold water run over it for an hour or so.

CAKED OR CLOGGED SALT
Tightly wrap a piece of aluminum foil around the salt shaker. This will keep the dampness out of the salt. To prevent clogging, keep 5 to 10 grains of rice inside your shaker.

SOGGY POTATO CHIPS, CEREAL AND CRACKERS
If potato chips lose their freshness, place under broiler for a few moments. Care must be taken not to brown them. You can crisp soggy cereal and crackers by putting them on a cookie sheet and heating for a few minutes in the oven.

PANCAKE SYRUP
To make an inexpensive syrup for pancakes, save small amounts of leftover jams and jellies in a jar. Or, fruit-flavored syrup can be made by adding 2 C. sugar to 1 C. of any kind of fruit juice and cooking until it boils.

EASY TOPPING
A good topping for gingerbread, coffeecake, etc., can easily be made by freezing the syrup from canned fruit and adding 1 T. of butter and 1 T. of lemon juice to 2 C. of syrup. Heat until bubbly, and thicken with 2 T. of flour.

TASTY CHEESE SANDWICHES
Toast cheese sandwiches in a frying pan lightly greased with bacon fat for a delightful new flavor.

HURRY-UP HAMBURGERS
Poke a hole in the middle of the patties while shaping them. The burgers will cook faster and the holes will disappear when done.

SHRINKLESS LINKS
Boil sausage links for about 8 minutes before frying and they will shrink less and not break at all. Or, you can roll them lightly in flour before frying.

FROZEN BREAD
Put frozen bread loaves in a clean brown paper bag and place for 5 minutes in a 325° oven to thaw completely.

REMOVING THE CORN SILK
Dampen a paper towel or terry cloth and brush downward on the cob of corn. Every strand should come off.

NUTS
To quickly crack open a large amount of nuts, put in a bag and gently hammer until they are cracked open. Then remove nutmeats with a pick.

If nuts are stale, place them in the oven at 250° and leave them there for 5 to 10 minutes. The heat will revive them.

PREVENTING BOIL-OVERS
Add a lump of butter or a few teaspoons of cooking oil to the water. Rice, noodles or spaghetti will not boil over or stick together.

SOFTENING BUTTER
Soften butter quickly by grating it. Or heat a small pan and place it upside-down over the butter dish for several minutes. Or place in the microwave for a few seconds.

MEASURING STICKY LIQUIDS
Before measuring honey or syrup, oil the cup with cooking oil and rinse in hot water.

SCALDED MILK
Add a bit of sugar (without stirring) to milk to prevent it from scorching.

Rinse the pan in cold water before scalding milk, and it will be much easier to clean.

TENDERIZING MEAT

Boiled meat: Add a tablespoon of vinegar to the cooking water.

Tough meat or game: Make a marinade of equal parts cooking vinegar and heated bouillon. Marinate for 2 hours.

Steak: Simply rub in a mixture of cooking vinegar and oil. Allow to stand for 2 hours.

Chicken: To stew an old hen, soak it in vinegar for several hours before cooking. It will taste like a spring chicken.

INSTANT WHITE SAUCE

Blend together 1 C. soft butter and 1 C. flour. Spread in an ice cube tray, chill well, cut into 16 cubes before storing in a plastic bag in the freezer. For medium-thick sauce, drop 1 cube into 1 C. of milk and heat slowly, stirring as it thickens.

UNPLEASANT COOKING ODORS

While cooking vegetables that give off unpleasant odors, simmer a small pan of vinegar on top of the stove. Or, add vinegar to the cooking water. To remove the odor of fish from cooking and serving implements, rinse in vinegar water.

DON'T LOSE THOSE VITAMINS

Put vegetables in water after the water boils - not before - to be sure to preserve all the vegetables' vitamins.

CLEAN AND DEODORIZE YOUR CUTTING BOARD

Bleach it clean with lemon juice. Take away strong odors like onion with baking soda. Just rub in.

KEEP THE COLOR IN BEETS

If you find that your beets tend to lose color when you boil them, add a little lemon juice.

NO-SMELL CABBAGE

Two things to do to keep cabbage smell from filling the kitchen; don't overcook it (keep it crisp) and put half a lemon in the water when you boil it.

A GREAT ENERGY SAVER
When you're near the end of the baking time, turn the oven off and keep the door closed. The heat will stay the same long enough to finish baking your cake or pie and you'll save all that energy.

GRATING CHEESE
Chill the cheese before grating and it will take much less time.

SPECIAL LOOKING PIES
Give a unique look to your pies by using pinking shears to cut the dough. Make a pinked lattice crust!

REMOVING HAM RIND
Before placing ham in the roasting pan, slit rind lengthwise on the underside. The rind will peel away as the ham cooks, and can be easily removed.

SLUGGISH CATSUP
Push a drinking straw to the bottom of the bottle and remove. This admits enough air to start the catsup flowing.

UNMOLDING GELATIN
Rinse the mold pan in cold water and coat with salad oil. The oil will give the gelatin a nice luster and it will easily fall out of the mold.

LEFTOVER SQUASH
Squash that is leftover can be improved by adding some maple syrup before reheated.

NO-SPILL CUPCAKES
An ice cream scoop can be used to fill cupcake papers without spilling.

SLICING CAKE OR TORTE
Use dental floss to slice evenly and cleanly through a cake or torte - simply stretch a length of the floss taut and press down through the cake.

CANNING PEACHES

Don't bother to remove skins when canning or freezing peaches. They will taste better and be more nutritious with the skin on.

ANGEL FOOD COOKIES

Stale angel food cake can be cut into ½-inch slices and shaped with cookie cutters to make delicious "cookies". Just toast in the oven for a few minutes.

HOW TO CHOP GARLIC

Chop in a small amount of salt to prevent pieces from sticking to the knife or chopping board then pulverize with the tip or the knife.

EXCESS FAT ON SOUPS OR STEWS

Remove fat from stews or soups by refrigerating and eliminating fat as it rises and hardens on the surface. Or add lettuce leaves to the pot - the fat will cling to them. Discard lettuce before serving.

BROILED MEAT DRIPPINGS

Place a piece of bread under the rack on which you are broiling meat. Not only will this absorb the dripping fat, but it will reduce the chance of the fat catching on fire.

FAKE SOUR CREAM

To cut down on calories, run cottage cheese through the blender. It can be flavored with chives, extracts, etc., and used in place of mayonnaise.

BROWNED BUTTER

Browning brings out the flavor of the butter, so only half as much is needed for seasoning vegetables if it is browned before it is added.

COOKING DRIED BEANS

When cooking dried beans, add salt after cooking; if salt is added at the start it will slow the cooking process.

TASTY CARROTS

Adding sugar and horseradish to cooked carrots improves their flavor.

CARROT MARINADE
Marinate carrot sticks in dill pickle juice.

CLEAN CUKES
A ball of nylon net cleans and smooths cucumbers when making pickles.

FRESH GARLIC
Peel garlic and store in a covered jar of vegetable oil. The garlic will stay fresh and the oil will be nicely flavored for salad dressings.

LEFTOVER WAFFLES
Freeze waffles that are left; they can be reheated in the toaster.

FLUFFY RICE
Rice will be fluffier and whiter if you add 1 tsp. of lemon juice to each quart of water.

NUTRITIOUS RICE
Cook rice in liquid saved from cooking vegetables to add flavor and nutrition. A nutty taste can be achieved by adding wheat germ to the rice.

PERFECT NOODLES
When cooking noodles, bring required amount of water to a boil, add noodles, turn heat off and allow to stand for 20 minutes. This prevents overboiling and the chore of stirring. Noodles won't stick to the pan with this method.

EASY CROUTONS
Make delicious croutons for soup or salad by saving toast, cutting into cubes, and sauteeing in garlic butter.

BAKED FISH
To keep fish from sticking to the pan, bake on a bed of chopped onion, celery and parsley. This also adds a nice flavor to the fish.

NON-STICKING BACON

Roll a package of bacon into a tube before opening. This will loosen the slices and keep them from sticking together.

TASTY HOT DOGS

Boil hot dogs in sweet pickle juice and a little water for a different tate.

GOLDEN-BROWN CHICKEN

For golden-brown fried chicken, roll it in powdered milk instead of flour.

DOUBLE BOILER HINT

Toss a few marbles in the bottom of a double boiler. When the water boils down, the noise will let you know!

FLOUR PUFF

Keep a powder puff in your flour container to easily dust your rolling pin or pastry board.

JAR LABELS

Attach canning labels to the lids instead of the sides of jelly jars, to prevent the chore of removing the labels when the contents are gone.

DIFFERENT MEATBALLS

Try using crushed corn flakes or corn bread instead of bread crumbs in a meatball recipe or use onion-flavored potato chips.

CLEAN-UP TIPS

APPLIANCES

To rid yellowing from white appliances try this. Mix together ½ C. bleach, ¼ C. baking soda, and 4 C. warm water. Apply with a sponge and let set for 10 minutes. Rinse and dry thoroughly.

Instead of using commercial waxes, shine with rubbing alcohol.

For quick clean-ups, rub with equal parts water and household ammonia.

Or, try club soda. It cleans and polishes at the same time.

BLENDER
Fill part way with hot water and add a drop of detergent. Cover and turn it on for a few seconds. Rinse and drain dry.

BREADBOARDS
To rid cutting board of onion, garlic or fish smell, cut a lime or lemon in two and rub the surface with the cut side of the fruit.

Or, make a paste of baking soda and water and apply generously. Rinse.

COPPER POTS
Fill a spray bottle with vinegar and add 3 T. of salt. Spray solution liberally on copper pot. Let set for awhile, then simply rub clean.

Dip lemon halves in salt and rub.

Or, rub with Worcestershire sauce or catsup. The tarnish will disappear.

Clean with toothpaste and rinse.

BURNT AND SCORCHED PANS
Sprinkle burnt pans liberally with baking soda, adding just enough water to moisten. Let stand for several hours. You can generally lift the burned portions right out of the pan.

Stubborn stains on non-stick cookware can be removed by boiling 2 T. of baking soda, ½ C. vinegar, and 1 C. water for 10 minutes. Re-season with salad oil.

CAST-IRON SKILLETS
Clean the outside of the pan with commercial oven cleaner. Let set for 2 hours and the accumulated black stains can be removed with vinegar and water.

CAN OPENER
Loosen grime by brushing with an old toothbrush. To thoroughly clean blades, run a paper towel through the cutting process.

ENAMELWARE CASSEROLE DISHES

Fill a dish that contains stuck food bits with boiling water and 2 T. of baking soda. Let it stand and wash out.

DISHES

Save time and money by using the cheapest brand of dishwashing detergent available, but add a few tablespoons of vinegar to the dishwasher. The vinegar will cut the grease and leave your dishes sparkling clean.

Before washing fine china and crystal, place a towel on the bottom of the sink to act as a cushion.

To remove coffee or tea stains and cigarette burns from fine china, rub with a damp cloth dipped in baking soda.

DISHWASHER

Run a cup of white vinegar through the entire cycle in an empty dishwasher to remove all soap film.

CLOGGED DRAINS

When a drain is clogged with grease, pour a cup of salt and a cup of baking soda into the drain followed by a kettle of boiling water. The grease will usually dissolve immediately and open the drain.

Coffee grounds are a no-no. They do a nice job of clogging, especially if they get mixed with grease.

GARBAGE DISPOSAL

Grind a half lemon or orange rind in the disposal to remove any unpleasant odor.

OVEN

Following a spill, sprinkle with salt immediately. When oven is cool, brush off burnt food and wipe with a damp sponge.

Sprinkle bottom of oven with automatic dishwasher soap and cover with wet paper towels. Let stand for a few hours.

A quick way to clean oven parts is to place a bath towel in the bathtub and pile all removable parts from the oven onto it. Draw enough hot water to just cover the parts and sprinkle a cup of dishwasher soap over it. While you are cleaning the inside of the oven, the rest will be cleaning itself.

An inexpensive oven cleaner. Set oven on warm for about 20 minutes, then turn off. Place a small dish of full strength ammonia on the top shelf. Put large pan of boiling water on the bottom shelf and let it set overnight. In the morning, open oven and let it air a while before washing off with soap and water. Even the hard baked-on grease will wash off easily.

PLASTIC CUPS, DISHES AND CONTAINERS
Coffee or tea stains can be scoured with baking soda.

Or, fill the stained cup with hot water and drop in a few denture cleanser tablets. Let soak for 1 hour.

To rid foul odors from plastic containers, place crumbled-up newspaper (black and white only) into the container. Cover tightly and leave overnight.

REFRIGERATOR
To help eliminate odors fill a small bowl with charcoal (the kind used for potted plants) and place it on a shelf in the refrigerator. It absorbs ordors rapidly.

An open box of baking soda will absorb food odors for at least a month or two.

A little vanilla poured on a piece of cotton and place in the refrigerator will eliminate odors.

To prevent mildew from forming, wipe with vinegar. The acid effectively kills the mildew fungus.

Use a glycerine-soaked cloth to wipe sides and shelves. Future spills wipe up easily. Add after the freezer has been defrosted, coat the inside coils with glycerine. The next time you defrost, the ice will loosen quickly and drop off in sheets.

Wash inside and out with a mixture of 3 T. of baking soda in a quart of warm water.

SINKS
For a sparkling white sink, place paper towels across the bottom of your sink and saturate with household bleach. Let set for ½ hour or so.

Rub stainless steel sinks with lighter fluid if rust marks appear. After the rust disappears, wipe with your regular kitchen cleanser.

Use a cloth dampened with rubbing alcohol to remove water spots from stainless steel.

Spots on stainless steel can also be removed with white vinegar.

Club soda will shine up stainless steel sinks in a jiffy.

SPONGES
Wash in your dishwasher or soak overnight in salt water or baking soda added to water.

THERMOS BOTTLE
Fill the bottle with warm water, add 1 tsp. of baking soda and allow to soak.

TIN PIE PANS
Remove rust by dipping a raw potato in cleaning powder and scouring.

FINGERPRINTS OFF THE KITCHEN DOOR AND WALLS
Take away fingerprints and grime with a solution of half water and half ammonia. Put it in a spray bottle from one of these expensive cleaning products, you'll never have to buy them again.

FORMICA TOPS
Polish them to a sparkle with club soda.

KEEPING FOODS FRESH AND FOOD STORAGE

CELERY AND LETTUCE
Store in refrigerator in paper bags instead of plastic. Leave the outside leaves and stalks on until ready to use.

ONIONS
Once an onion has been cut in half, rub the leftover side with butter and it will keep fresh longer.

CHEESE
Wrap cheese in a vinegar-dampened cloth to keep it from drying out.

MILK
Milk at room temperature may spoil cold milk, so don't pour milk back into the carton.

BROWN SUGAR
Wrap in a plastic bag and store in refrigerator in a coffee can with a snap-on lid.

COCOA
Store cocoa in a glass jar in a dry and cool place.

CAKES
Putting half an apple in the cake box will keep cake moist.

ICE CREAM
Ice cream that has been opened and returned to the freezer sometimes forms a waxlike film on the top. To prevent this, after part of the ice cream has been removed press a piece of waxed paper against the surface and reseal the carton.

LEMONS
Store whole lemons in a tightly sealed jar of water in the refrigerator. They will yield much more juice than when first purchased.

LIMES
Store limes, wrapped in tissue paper, on lower shelf of the refrigerator.

SMOKED MEATS
Wrap ham or bacon in vinegar-soaked cloth, then in waxed paper to preserve freshness.

STRAWBERRIES
Keep in a colander in the refrigerator. Wash just before serving.

(200)

NOTES

NOTES

Since you have enjoyed this book, perhaps you would be interested in some of these others from QUIXOTE PRESS.

ARKANSAS BOOKS

HOW TO TALK ARKANSAS
        by Bruce Carlson .... paperback $7.95
ARKANSAS' ROADKILL COOKBOOK
        by Bruce Carlson .... paperback $7.95
REVENGE OF ROADKILL
        by Bruce Carlson .... paperback $7.95
GHOSTS OF THE OZARKS
        by Bruce Carlson .... paperback $9.95
A FIELD GUIDE TO SMALL ARKANSAS FEMALES
        by Bruce Carlson .... paperback $9.95
LET'S US GO DOWN TO THE RIVER 'N...
        by various authors .... paperback $9.95
ARKANSAS' VANISHING OUTHOUSE
        by Bruce Carlson .... paperback $9.95
TALL TALES OF THE MISSISSIPPI RIVER
        by Dan Titus .... paperback $9.95
LOST & BURIED TREASURE OF THE MISSISSIPPI RIVER
        by Netha Bell & Gary Scholl .... paperback $9.95
TALES OF HACKETT'S CREEK
        by Dan Titus .... paperback $9.95
UNSOLVED MYSTERIES OF THE MISSISSIPPI RIVER
        by Netha Bell .... paperback $9.95
101 WAYS TO USE A DEAD RIVER FLY
        by Bruce Carlson .... paperback $7.95
VACANT LOT, SCHOOL YARD & BACK ALLEY GAMES
        by various authors .... paperback $9.95
HOW TO TALK MIDWESTERN
        by Robert Thomas .... paperback $7.95
ARKANSAS COOKIN'
        by Bruce Carlson .... (3x5) paperback $5.95

DAKOTA BOOKS

HOW TO TALK DAKOTA .... paperback $7.95
Some Pretty Tame, but Kinda Funny Stories About Early
DAKOTA LADIES-OF-THE-EVENING
        by Bruce Carlson .... paperback $9.95

SOUTH DAKOTA ROADKILL COOKBOOK
by Bruce Carlson .... paperback $7.95
REVENGE OF ROADKILL
by Bruce Carlson .... paperback $7.95
101 WAYS TO USE A DEAD RIVER FLY
by Bruce Carlson .... paperback $7.95
LET'S US GO DOWN TO THE RIVER 'N...
by various authors .... paperback $9.95
LOST & BURIED TREASURE OF THE MISSOURI RIVER
by Netha Bell .... paperback $9.95
MAKIN' DO IN SOUTH DAKOTA
by various authors .... paperback $9.95
GUNSHOOTIN', WHISKEY DRINKIN', GIRL CHASIN' STORIES
OUT OF THE OLD DAKOTAS
by Netha Bell .... paperback $9.95
THE DAKOTAS' VANISHING OUTHOUSE
by Bruce Carlson .... paperback $9.95
VACANT LOT, SCHOOL YARD & BACK ALLEY GAMES
by various authors .... paperback $9.95
HOW TO TALK MIDWESTERN
by Robert Thomas .... paperback $7.95
DAKOTA COOKIN'
by Bruce Carlson .... (3x5) paperback $5.95

ILLINOIS BOOKS

ILLINOIS COOKIN'
by Bruce Carlson .... (3x5) paperback $5.95
THE VANISHING OUTHOUSE OF ILLINOIS
by Bruce Carlson .... paperback $9.95
A FIELD GUIDE TO ILLINOIS' CRITTERS
by Bruce Carlson .... paperback $7.95
YOU KNOW YOU'RE IN ILLINOIS WHEN...
by Bruce Carlson .... paperback $7.95
Some Pretty Tame, but Kinda Funny Stories About Early
ILLINOIS LADIES-OF-THE-EVENING
by Bruce Carlson .... paperback $9.95
ILLINOIS' ROADKILL COOKBOOK
by Bruce Carlson .... paperback $7.95
101 WAYS TO USE A DEAD RIVER FLY
by Bruce Carlson .... paperback $7.95

HOW TO TALK ILLINOIS
     by Netha Bell .... paperback $7.95
TALL TALES OF THE MISSISSIPPI RIVER
     by Dan Titus .... paperback $9.95
TALES OF HACKETT'S CREEK
     by Dan Titus .... paperback $9.95
UNSOLVED MYSTERIES OF THE MISSISSIPPI
     by Netha Bell .... paperback $9.95
LOST & BURIED TREASURE OF THE MISSISSIPPI RIVER
     by Netha Bell & Gary Scholl .... paperback $9.95
STRANGE FOLKS ALONG THE MISSISSIPPI
     by Pat Wallace .... paperback $9.95
LET'S US GO DOWN TO THE RIVER 'N...
     by various authors .... paperback $9.95
MISSISSIPPI RIVER PO' FOLK
     by Pat Wallace .... paperback $9.95
GHOSTS OF THE MISSISSIPPI RIVER (from Keokuk to St. Louis)
     by Bruce Carlson .... paperback $9.95
GHOSTS OF THE MISSISSIPPI RIVER (from Dubuque to Keokuk)
     by Bruce Carlson .... paperback $9.95
MAKIN' DO IN ILLINOIS
     by various authors .... paperback $9.95
MY VERY FIRST
     by various authors .... paperback $9.95
VACANT LOT, SCHOOL YARD & BACK ALLEY GAMES
     by various authors .... paperback $9.95
HOW TO TALK MIDWESTERN
     by Robert Thomas .... paperback $7.95

INDIANA BOOKS

HOW TO TALK INDIANA .... paperback $7.95
INDIANA'S ROADKILL COOKBOOK
     by Bruce Carlson .... paperback $7.95
REVENGE OF ROADKILL
     by Bruce Carlson .... paperback $7.95
A FIELD GUIDE TO SMALL INDIANA FEMALES
     by Bruce Carlson .... paperback $9.95
GHOSTS OF THE OHIO RIVER (from Cincinnati to Louisville)
     by Bruce Carlson .... paperback $9.95
LET'S US GO DOWN TO THE RIVER 'N...
     by various authors .... paperback $9.95

101 WAYS TO USE A DEAD RIVER FLY
     by Bruce Carlson .... paperback $7.95
INDIANA'S VARNISHING OUTHOUSE
     by Bruce Carlson .... paperback $9.95
VACANT LOT, SCHOOL YARD & BACK ALLEY GAMES
     by various authors .... paperback $9.95
HOW TO TALK MIDWESTERN
     by Robert Thomas .... paperback $7.95

· IOWA BOOKS

IOWA COOKIN'
     by Bruce Carlson .... (3x5) paperback $5.95
IOWA'S ROADKILL COOKBOOK
     By Bruce Carlson .... paperback $7.95
REVENGE OF ROADKILL
     by Bruce Carlson .... paperback $7.95
IOWA'S OLD SCHOOLHOUSES
     by Carole Turner Johnston .... paperback $9.95
GHOSTS OF THE AMANA COLONIES
     by Lori Erickson .... paperback $9.95
GHOSTS OF THE IOWA GREAT LAKES
     by Bruce Carlson .... paperback $9.95
GHOSTS OF THE MISSISSIPPI RIVER (from Dubuque to Keokuk)
     by Bruce Carlson .... paperback $9.95
GHOSTS OF THE MISSISSIPPI RIVER (from Minneapolis to Dubuque)
     by Bruce Carlson .... paperback $9.95
GHOSTS OF POLK COUNTY, IOWA
     by Tom Welch .... paperback $9.95
TALES OF HACKETT'S CREEK
     by Dan Titus .... paperback $9.95
ME 'N WESLEY (stories about the homemade toys that
  Iowa farm children made and played with around the turn of the century)
     by Bruce Carlson .... paperback $9.95
TALL TALES OF THE MISSISSIPPI RIVER.
     by Dan Titus .... paperback $9.95
HOW TO TALK IOWA .... paperback $7.95
UNSOLVED MYSTERIES OF THE MISSISSIPPI
     by Netha Bell .... paperback $9.95
101 WAYS TO USE A DEAD RIVER FLY
     by Bruce Carlson .... paperback $7.95

LET'S US GO DOWN TO THE RIVER 'N...
        by various authors .... paperback $9.95
TRICKS WE PLAYED IN IOWA
        by various authors .... paperback $9.95
IOWA, THE LAND BETWEEN THE VOWELS
  (farm boy stories from the early 1900s)
        by Bruce Carlson .... paperback $9.95
LOST & BURIED TREASURE OF THE MISSISSIPPI RIVER
        by Netha Bell & Gary Scholl .... paperback $9.95
Some Pretty Tame, but Kinda Funny Stories About Early
IOWA LADIES-OF-THE-EVENING
        by Bruce Carlson .... paperback $9.95
THE VANISHING OUTHOUSE OF IOWA
        by Bruce Carlson .... paperback $9.95
IOWA'S EARLY HOME REMEDIES
        by 26 students at Wapello Elem. School .... paperback $9.95
IOWA - A JOURNEY IN A PROMISED LAND
        by Kathy Yoder .... paperback $16.95
LOST & BURIED TREASURE OF THE MISSOURI RIVER
        by Netha Bell .... paperback $9.95
FIELD GUIDE TO IOWA'S CRITTERS
        by Bruce Carlson .... paperback $7.95
OLD IOWA HOUSES, YOUNG LOVES
        by Bruce Carlson .... paperback $9.95
SKUNK RIVER ANTHOLOGY
        by Gene Olson .... paperback $9.95
VACANT LOT, SCHOOL YARD & BACK ALLEY GAMES
        by various authors .... paperback $9.95
HOW TO TALK MIDWESTERN
        by Robert Thomas .... paperback $7.95

KANSAS BOOKS

HOW TO TALK KANSAS .... paperback $7.95
STOPOVER IN KANSAS
        by Jon McAlpin .... paperback $9.95
LET'S US GO DOWN TO THE RIVER 'N ...
        by various authors .... paperback $9.95
LOST & BURIED TREASURE OF THE MISSOURI RIVER
        by Netha Bell .... paperback $9.95

101 WAYS TO USE A DEAD RIVER FLY
     by Bruce Carlson .... paperback $7.95
VACANT LOT, SCHOOL YARD & BACK ALLEY GAMES
     by various authors .... paperback $9.95
HOW TO TALK MIDWESTERN
     by Robert Thomas .... paperback $7.95

KENTUCKY BOOKS

GHOSTS OF THE OHIO RIVER (from Pittsburgh to Cincinnati)
     by Bruce Carlson .... paperback $9.95
GHOSTS OF THE OHIO RIVER (from Cincinnati to Louisville)
     by Bruce Carlson .... paperback $9.95
TALES OF HACKETT'S CREEK
     by Dan Titus .... paperback $9.95
LOST & BURIED TREASURE OF THE MISSISSIPPI RIVER
     by Netha Bell & Gary Scholl .... paperback $9.95
LET'S US GO DOWN TO THE RIVER 'N ...
     by various authors .... paperback $9.95
UNSOLVED MYSTERIES OF THE MISSISSIPPI
     by Netha Bell .... paperback $9.95
101 WAYS TO USE A DEAD RIVER FLY
     by Bruce Carlson .... paperback $7.95
TALL TALES OF THE MISSISSIPPI RIVER
     by Dan Titus .... paperback $9.95
MY VERY FIRST
     by various authors .... paperback $9.95
VACANT LOT, SCHOOL YARD & BACK ALLEY GAMES
     by various authors .... paperback $9.95

MICHIGAN BOOKS

MICHIGAN COOKIN'
     by Bruce Carlson .... (3x5) paperback $5.95
MICHIGAN'S ROADKILL COOKBOOK
     by Bruce Carlson .... paperback $7.95
MICHIGAN'S VANISHING OUTHOUSE
     by Bruce Carlson .... paperback $9.95

MINNESOTA BOOKS

MINNESOTA'S ROADKILL COOKBOOK
     by Bruce Carlson .... paperback $7.95
REVENGE OF ROADKILL
     by Bruce Carlson .... paperback $7.95
A FIELD GUIDE TO SMALL MINNESOTA FEMALES
     by Bruce Carlson .... paperback $9.95
GHOSTS OF THE MISSISSIPPI RIVER (from Minneapolis to Dubuque)
     by Bruce Carlson .... paperback $9.95
LAKES COUNTRY COOKBOOK
     by Bruce Carlson .... paperback $11.95
UNSOLVED MYSTERIES OF THE MISSISSIPPI
     by Netha Bell .... paperback $9.95
TALES OF HACKETT'S CREEK
     by Dan Titus .... paperback $9.95
GHOSTS OF SOUTHWEST MINNESOTA
     by Ruth Hein .... paperback $9.95
HOW TO TALK LIKE A MINNESOTA NATIVE .... paperback $7.95
MINNESOTA'S VANISHING OUTHOUSE
     by Bruce Carlson .... paperback $9.95
TALL TALES OF THE MISSISSIPPI RIVER
     by Dan Titus .... paperback $9.95
Some Pretty Tame, but Kinda Funny Stories About Early
MINNESOTA LADIES-OF-THE-EVENING
     by Bruce Carlson .... paperback $9.95
101 WAYS TO USE A DEAD RIVER FLY .... paperback $7.95
LOST & BURIED TREASURE OF THE MISSISSIPPI RIVER
     by Netha Bell & Gary Scholl .... paperback $9.95
VACANT LOT, SCHOOL YARD & BACK ALLEY GAMES
     by various authors .... paperback $9.95
HOW TO TALK MIDWESTERN
     by Robert Thomas .... paperback $7.95
MINNESOTA COOKIN'
     by Bruce Carlson .... (3x5) paperback $5.95

MISSOURI BOOKS

MISSOURI COOKIN'
     by Bruce Carlson .... (3x5) paperback $5.95
MISSOURI'S ROADKILL COOKBOOK
     by Bruce Carlson .... paperback $7.95

REVENGE OF ROADKILL
    by Bruce Carlson .... paperback $7.95
LET'S US GO DOWN TO THE RIVER 'N ...
    by various authors .... paperback $9.95
LAKES COUNTRY COOKBOOK
    by Bruce Carlson .... paperback $11.95
101 WAYS TO USE A DEAD RIVER FLY
    by Bruce Carlson .... paperback $7.95
TALL TALES OF THE MISSISSIPPI RIVER
    by Dan Titus .... paperback $9.95
TALES OF HACKETT'S CREEK
    by Dan Titus .... paperback $9.95
STRANGE FOLKS ALONG THE MISSISSIPPI
    by Pat Wallace .... paperback $9.95
LOST & BURIED TREASURE OF THE MISSOURI RIVER
    by Netha Bell .... paperback $9.95
HOW TO TALK MISSOURIAN
    by Bruce Carlson .... paperback $7.95
VACANT LOT, SCHOOL YARD & BACK ALLEY GAMES
    by various authors .... paperback $9.95
HOW TO TALK MIDWESTERN
    by Robert Thomas .... paperback $7.95
UNSOLVED MYSTERIES OF THE MISSISSIPPI
    by Netha Bell .... paperback $9.95
LOST & BURIED TREASURE OF THE MISSISSIPPI RIVER
    by Netha Bell & Gary Scholl .... paperback $9.95
MISSISSIPPI RIVER PO' FOLK
    by Pat Wallace .... paperback $9.95
Some Pretty Tame, but Kinda Funny Stories About Early
MISSOURI LADIES-OF-THE-EVENING
    by Bruce Carlson .... paperback $9.95
GUNSHOOTIN', WHISKEY DRINKIN', GIRL CHASIN'
STORIES OUT OF THE OLD MISSOURI TERRITORY
    by Bruce Carlson .... paperback $9.95
THE VANISHING OUTHOUSE OF MISSOURI
    by Bruce Carlson .... paperback $9.95
A FIELD GUIDE TO MISSOURI'S CRITTERS
    by Bruce Carlson .... paperback $7.95
EARLY MISSOURI HOME REMEDIES
    by various authors .... paperback $9.95
GHOSTS OF THE OZARKS
    by Bruce Carlson .... paperback $9.95

MISSISSIPPI RIVER COOKIN' BOOK
    by Bruce Carlson .... paperback $11.95
MISSOURI'S OLD HOUSES, AND NEW LOVES
    by Bruce Carlson .... paperback $9.95
UNDERGROUND MISSOURI
    by Bruce Carlson .... paperback $9.95

NEBRASKA BOOKS

LOST & BURIED TREASURE OF THE MISSOURI RIVER
    by Netha Bell .... paperback $9.95
101 WAYS TO USE A DEAD RIVER FLY
    by Bruce Carlson .... paperback $7.95
LET'S US GO DOWN TO THE RIVER 'N ...
    by various authors .... paperback $9.95
HOW TO TALK MIDWESTERN
    by Robert Thomas .... paperback $7.95
VACANT LOT, SCHOOL YARD & BACK ALLEY GAMES
    by various authors .... paperback $9.95

TENNESSEE BOOKS

TALES OF HACKETT'S CREED
    by Dan Titus .... paperback $9.95
TALL TALES OF THE MISSISSIPPI RIVER
    by Dan Titus .... paperback $9.95
UNSOLVED MYSTERIES OF THE MISSISSIPPI
    by Netha Bell .... paperback $9.95
LOST & BURIED TREASURE OF THE MISSISSIPPI RIVER
    by Netha Bell & Gary Scholl .... paperback $9.95
LET'S US GO DOWN TO THE RIVER 'N ...
    by various authors .... paperback $9.95
101 WAYS TO USE A DEAD RIVER FLY
    by Bruce Carlson .... paperback $7.95
VACANT LOT, SCHOOL YARD & BACK ALLEY GAMES
    by various authors .... paperback $9.95

HOW TO TALK WISCONSIN .... paperback $7.95
WISCONSIN COOKIN'
    by Bruce Carlson .... (3x5) paperback $5.95
WISCONSIN'S ROADKILL COOKBOOK
    by Bruce Carlson .... paperback $7.95
REVENGE OF ROADKILL
    by Bruce Carlson .... paperback $7.95
TALL TALES OF THE MISSISSIPPI RIVER
    by Dan Titus .... paperback $9.95
LAKES COUNTRY COOKBOOK
    by Bruce Carlson .... paperback $11.95
TALES OF HACKETT'S CREEK
    by Dan Titus .... paperback $9.95
LET'S US GO DOWN TO THE RIVER 'N ...
    by various authors .... paperback $9.95
101 WAYS TO USE A DEAD RIVER FLY
    by Bruce Carlson .... paperback $7.95
UNSOLVED MYSTERIES OF THE MISSISSIPPI
    by Netha Bell .... paperback $9.95
LOST & BURIED TREASURE OF THE MISSISSIPPI RIVER
    by Netha Bell & Gary Scholl .... paperback $9.95
GHOSTS OF THE MISSISSIPPI RIVER (from Dubuque to Keokuk)
    by Bruce Carlson .... paperback $9.95
HOW TO TALK MIDWESTERN
    by Robert Thomas .... paperback $7.95
VACANT LOT, SCHOOL YARD & BACK ALLEY GAMES
    by various authors .... paperback $9.95
MY VERY FIRST
    by various authors .... paperback $9.95
EARLY WISCONSIN HOME REMEDIES
    by various authors .... paperback $9.95
GHOSTS OF THE MISSISSIPPI RIVER (from Minneapolis to Dubuque)
    by Bruce Carlson .... paperback $9.95
THE VANISHING OUTHOUSE OF WISCONSIN
    by Bruce Carlson .... paperback $9.95
GHOSTS OF DOOR COUNTY, WISCONSIN
    by Geri Rider .... paperback $9.95
Some Pretty Tame, but Kinda Funny Stories About Early
WISCONSIN LADIES-OF-THE-EVENING
    by Bruce Carlson .... paperback $9.95

MIDWESTERN BOOKS

A FIELD GUIDE TO THE MIDWEST'S WORST RESTAURANTS
       by Bruce Carlson .... paperback $5.95
THE MOTORIST'S FIELD GUIDE TO MIDWESTERN FARM
EQUIPMENT (misguided information as only a city slicker can give it)
       by Bruce Carlson .... paperback $5.95
VACANT LOT, SCHOOL YARD & BACK ALLEY GAMES
OF THE MIDWEST YEARS AGO
       by various authors .... paperback $9.95
MIDWEST SMALL TOWN COOKING
       by Bruce Carlson .... (3x5) paperback $5.95
HITCHHIKING THE UPPER MIDWEST
       by Bruce Carlson .... paperback $7.95
101 WAYS FOR MIDWESTERNERS TO "DO IN" THEIR
NEIGHBOR'S PESKY DOG WITHOUT GETTING CAUGHT
       by Bruce Carlson .... paperback $5.95

RIVER BOOKS

ON THE SHOULDERS OF A GIANT
       by M. Cody and D. Walker .... paperback $9.95
SKUNK RIVER ANTHOLOGY
       by Gene "Will" Olson .... paperback $9.95
JACK KING vs. DETECTIVE MACKENZIE
       by Netha Bell .... paperback $9.95
LOST & BURIED TREASURES ALONG THE MISSISSIPPI
       by Netha Bell & Gary Scholl .... paperback $9.95
MISSISSIPPI RIVER PO' FOLK
       by Pat Wallace .... paperback $9.95
STRANGE FOLKS ALONG THE MISSISSIPPI
       by Pat Wallace .... paperback $9.95
GHOSTS OF THE OHIO RIVER (from Pittsburgh to Cincinnati)
       by Bruce Carlson .... paperback $9.95
GHOSTS OF THE OHIO RIVER (from Cincinnati to Louisville)
       by Bruce Carlson .... paperback $9.95
GHOSTS OF THE MISSISSIPPI RIVER (Minneapolis to Dubuque)
       by Bruce Carlson .... paperback $9.95
GHOSTS OF THE MISSISSIPPI RIVER (Dubuque to Keokuk)
       by Bruce Carlson .... paperback $9.95
TALL TALES OF THE MISSISSIPPI RIVER
       by Dan Titus .... paperback $9.95

TALL TALES OF THE MISSOURI RIVER
  by Dan Titus .... paperback $9.95
RIVER SHARKS & SHENANIGANS
  (tales of riverboat gambling of years ago)
  by Netha Bell .... paperback $9.95
UNSOLVED MYSTERIES OF THE MISSISSIPPI
  by Netha Bell .... paperback $9.95
TALES OF HACKETT'S CREEK (1940s Mississippi River kids)
  by Dan Titus .... paperback $9.95
101 WAYS TO USE A DEAD RIVER FLY
  by Bruce Carlson .... paperback $7.95
LET'S US GO DOWN TO THE RIVER 'N ...
  by various authors .... paperback $9.95
LOST & BURIED TREASURE OF THE MISSOURI
  by Netha Bell .... paperback $9.95

COOKBOOKS

ROARING 20's COOKBOOK
  by Bruce Carlson .... paperback $11.95
DEPRESSION COOKBOOK
  by Bruce Carlson .... paperback $11.95
LAKES COUNTRY COOKBOOK
  by Bruce Carlson .... paperback $11.95
A COOKBOOK FOR THEM WHAT AIN'T DONE A LOT OF COOKIN'
  by Bruce Carlson .... paperback $11.95
FLAT-OUT DIRT-CHEAP COOKIN' COOKBOOK
  by Bruce Carlson .... paperback $11.95
APHRODISIAC COOKING
  by Bruce Carlson .... paperback $11.95
WILD CRITTER COOKBOOK
  by Bruce Carlson .... paperback $11.95
I GOT FUNNIER-THINGS-TO-DO-THAN-COOKIN' COOKBOOK
  by Louise Lum .... paperback $11.95
MISSISSIPPI RIVER COOKIN' BOOK
  by Bruce Carlson .... paperback $11.95
HUNTING IN THE NUDE COOKBOOK
  by Bruce Carlson .... paperback $9.95
DAKOTA COOKIN'
  by Bruce Carlson .... (3x5) paperback $5.95
IOWA COOKIN'
  by Bruce Carlson .... (3x5) paperback $5.95

MICHIGAN COOKIN'
        by Bruce Carlson .... (3x5) paperback $5.95
MINNESOTA COOKIN'
        by Bruce Carlson .... (3x5) paperback $5.95
MISSOURI COOKIN'
        by Bruce Carlson .... (3x5) paperback $5.95
ILLINOIS COOKIN'
        by Bruce Carlson .... (3x5) paperback $5.95
WISCONSIN COOKIN'
        by Bruce Carlson .... (3x5) paperback $5.95
HILL COUNTRY COOKIN'
        by Bruce Carlson .... (3x5) paperback $5.95
MIDWEST SMALL TOWN COOKIN'
        by Bruce Carlson .... (3x5) paperback $5.95
APHRODISIAC COOKIN'
        by Bruce Carlson .... (3x5) paperback $5.95
PREGNANT LADY COOKIN'
        by Bruce Carlson .... (3x5) paperback $5.95
GOOD COOKIN' FROM THE PLAIN PEOPLE
        by Bruce Carlson .... (3x5) paperback $5.95
WORKING GIRL COOKING
        by Bruce Carlson .... (3x5) paperback $5.95
COOKING FOR ONE
        by Barb Layton .... paperback $11.95
SUPER SIMPLE COOKING
        by Barb Layton .... (3x5) paperback $5.95
OFF TO COLLEGE COOKBOOK
        by Barb Layton .... (3x5) paperback $5.95
COOKING WITH THINGS THAT GO SPLASH
        by Bruce Carlson .... (3x5) paperback $5.95
COOKING WITH THINGS THAT GO MOO
        by Bruce Carlson .... (3x5) paperback $5.95
COOKING WITH SPIRITS
        by Bruce Carlson .... (3x5) paperback $5.95
INDIAN COOKING COOKBOOK
        by Bruce Carlson .... paperback $9.95
DIAL-A-DREAM COOKBOOK
        by Bruce Carlson .... (3x5) paperback $5.95
HORMONE HELPER COOKBOOK .... (3x5) paperback $5.95

MISCELLANEOUS BOOKS

DEAR TABBY (letters to and from a feline advice columnist)
by Bruce Carlson .... paperback $5.95
HOW TO BEHAVE (etiquette advice for non-traditional
and awkward circumstances such as attending dogfights,
what to do when your blind date turns out to be your spouse, etc.)
by Bruce Carlson .... paperback $5.95
REVENGE OF THE ROADKILL
by Bruce Carlson .... paperback $7.95